LOOK OUT AMERICA!

LOOK OUT AMERICA!

OUR U.S. AUTO INDUSTRY
IS LIVING ON BORROWED TIME

BY DEL C. SCHROEDER

LOOKOUTAMERICA.ORG, 2011

*I dedicate this book to my wife Jan,
the love of my life.*

TABLE OF CONTENTS

LOOK OUT AMERICA!

INTRODUCTION

We are not afraid to entrust the American people with unpleasant facts, foreign ideas, alien philosophies, and competitive values. For a nation that is afraid to let its people judge the truth and falsehood in an open market is a nation that is afraid of its people. —John F. Kennedy, 35th U.S. President (1917-1963)

On September 20, 2010, The National Bureau of Economic Research (NBER) declared that the longest recession since the Great Depression had officially ended in June, 2009. That was the same month that General Motor's declared bankruptcy. Those people that still remain unemployed do not believe the government fully understands their plight, and "The End of the Recession" message was just to make people feel good.

I AM A POSITIVE UPBEAT PERSON. All my life, I have always tried to find the bright side of the situation. As I've become older, my vision is much more realistic and pragmatic on the potential outcome of a situation. Case in point: I believe that in the next 18 months there could be a global contraction of spending. I project starting in mid- to late 2011, the business cycles all start diving for the bottom of the trough, and hitting bottom in 2012. In June, 2011, investors are beginning to see a weakening in the stock market. The United States of America could be entering the first depression of the 21st century as a Black Swan Event.

The economy clearly just hit a brick wall. —Paul Ashworth, Chief United States Economist at Capital Economics. (The New York Times, June 4, 2011.)

Black Swans are unpredictable events that are vulnerable to the contagion of fear—the reason why it destroys prediction models. My Black Swan prediction for a full-scale depression for 2012 is definitely an anomaly, and a situation the auto industry must be prepared for as a worst-case scenario.

The National Debt has continued to increase an average of $4.10 billion per day since September 28, 2007!

This Black Swan Event could very possibly complete the de-industrialization of America in one fell swoop, and make the United States the first post-World War II nation without an industrial base.

WHY NOW?

It seems like everyone in the United States has been living like there is no tomorrow. Many have all over-borrowed, whether it be personal, business, city, state or national government. Many seem to be over-extended. The amount of debt racked up by the forementioned groups is in the process of becoming overwhelming. What the United States is going through economically has been accruing over many years.

In the year 2011, the national debt will increase another 1.2 trillion dollars, or more, depending on what the Republicans in Congress will approve.

I AM AN AMERICAN CITIZEN who cares what happens to this once great country of ours. I'm not concerned about me because I have now reached the age where I can brag about it—I'm 73. But I'm concerned for my children and my grandchildren, and also for the readers' children and grandchildren. I have tried not to mince words to be politically correct; I just tried to present the picture as I see it to help turn this country around and let the readers form their own opinion on what needs to be done and how to survive a Black Swan Event, when it occurs.

The purpose of *Look Out America* is to give warning before it is too late. Ford and General Motors need to prepare a Black Swan scenario for how the last, two American auto companies can cope, and what they can do to survive in 2012 and beyond.

Look Out America also intends to provide a spiritual leadership solution to the structural problem plaguing the American auto industry today. The current mentality is constant reorganization as the cure to all fix all ills. No one understands how important it is to capture the employees' hearts, minds and souls before they are moved around in reorganizational changes.

Auto industry employees are looking for leadership that provides a vision of where the company is going and how they are going to get there. It is the character of the company that inspires confidence in the employees to give the best they can give. Structural solutions (reorganization) do nothing to solve spiritual problems. Employees are looking for inspirational leadership to navigate the companies out of a despairing situation.

AS A YOUNG MAN, I was always intrigued by creativity, innovation and new technology. To become competitive again, it will take good, old Yankee Ingenuity plus the commitment of everyone at Ford and GM to support creativity, innovation and technology. Creative solutions are needed to make the paradigm shift from the current way of doing business—*Look Out America* points the way.

The last, two American auto companies can survive the First Great Depression of the 21st century by producing vehicles that provide value to customers.

Now that Chrysler is part of the Fiat Group of Italy, I considered Chrysler/Fiat to be a foreign auto company with engineering and manufacturing operations in the United States, just like Toyota and Nissan.

SOMETIMES WE ARE SO CLOSE TO THE SITUATION we don't even realize the gravity until it's too late. But to me, the reality of life in America has been in a slow, gradual backward slide toward mediocrity over the past forty or so years—the same amount of time it took the Detroit auto industry to move from leading the world auto industry in 1968 to appearing before Congress hoping for a government handout in 2008.

It appears to me the health and prosperity of the United States as a nation parallels the health and prosperity of the American auto industry. The prosperity of a nation is built on the prosperity of its industrial base, plain and simple. Without industry there is no prosperity! Yet, hardly anyone in the United States government has the faintest clue how the two interact. For every major industrial job created there are a multitude of jobs created to support each job. Asian countries know this all too well, which is why they displace their unemployment to the United States every time they ship products to America.

Industry builds and creates products from raw materials. Service businesses provide services, like washing dishes. There is no way on God's Green Earth a nation the size of the United States can support a welfare society, illegal immigrants, a war in Afghanistan, and military superpower strength with bases all over the world with a service economy based on borrowed money.

Remember, in the marketplace each American auto company is on their own. They are competing with each other and also with Japan Inc., Korea Inc., Germany Inc., and China Inc. All foreign companies have some indirect support from their parent country. Of course, most countries want a piece of the American auto industry pie because it's their jobs and economy at stake.

Think of it, the Middle East, Korea, Japan, and China have it all figured out and are eating our lunch, thinking, "Stupid Americans." It does not take a rocket scientist to figure out where the outflow of our money is going.

In 1961 the United States was a rich and an industrious nation. Today, 50 years later, the United States has neither money nor industry.

> *And so, my fellow Americans, ask not what your country*
> *can do for you; ask what you can do for your country.*
> *—John F. Kennedy*

And that's the key. It's time we pull ourselves up by the bootstraps. It's time we help ourselves before it's too late. Ford and General Motors can take the lead in returning quality and creatively foreward-thinking manufacturing to American shores.

Del C. Schroeder

PART ONE: STRATEGIC PLANNING

WHAT WENT WRONG WITH DETROIT

THE BLACK SWAN

THE U.S. NEEDS A STRATEGIC PLAN

CONSOLIDATION AND A STRATEGIC PLAN FOR THE AMERICAN AUTO INDUSTRY

WHAT WENT WRONG WITH DETROIT

A great corporation is never conquered by the competition, until it has first destroyed itself from within. —Del C. Schroeder

When traveling around the country, engaging with business, military and academic people who have no connection—other than as customers—with the automotive industry, the question is inevitably asked, "What went wrong with Detroit?" To answer that question, both external and internal factors must be considered.

EXTERNAL FACTORS

Let's look at the externals first, because some are deeply embedded in American history or culture. It can be argued that three principal externals bedeviled Detroit. The first, dating to Colonial days, is the agricultural focus of the American government to the virtual exclusion of manufacturing. The second, barely more than a century in development, is an institutional anti-business bias by government, mass media, and other cultural elites. The third is the curse, especially in hard times, of quarterly financial reports that distinguish Detroit companies from their European and Asian competitors.

Agricultural and Land Focus

Our agricultural slant dates back to the British North American Colonies of the 17th and 18th centuries, when the Crown's policy was to hand out land grants and prohibit any manufacturing which might compete with the home industries. When the yoke of the King was thrown off in the American Revolution though, the bias toward land and agriculture continued.

Our new government honored the Royal grants of lands predating the Revolution, and the United States of America owned most of what was left, namely what came to be called the Northwest Territories—that part of the continent west of Pennsylvania, north of the Ohio River and east of the Mississippi. One of the first acts of our new Congress was to pass the Northwest Ordinance of 1787 and authorize the land obtained in the settlement with England to be carved up into neat, square townships.

For decades, the U. S. government's principal revenue came from selling those lands to pioneers and others on the march westward. The federal government underwrote the construction of canals in the East and Midwest to move settlers and goods westward and farm produce eastward. In the middle of the 19th century, the government's agricultural support switched from canals to railroads, which were granted alternate land sections along proposed rights-of-way to encourage the westward flow of people and goods. As domestic manufacturing industry grew east of the Mississippi, it was rarely supported by government subsidy.

Today, we can look back at over 100 years of Secretaries of Agriculture in the Presidential Cabinet, and a huge bureaucratic Agricultural Department established by President Lincoln, but never a Secretary of Industry or, specifically, Technology. There are agricultural subsidies galore, and huge agricultural corporations have become beneficiaries of congressional actions originally aimed at preserving the family farm. Witness those still pouring from Washington into tobacco farming (or not farming as the case may be) at the same time other agencies have done their best to eliminate the tobacco industry. The latest beneficiary of Washington's support is the ready promotion of corn-based ethanol to offset imported petroleum, despite arguments by experts that its costs outweigh its benefits.

In contrast, feudal Europe never had much land available for "family farming," as most property was owned by the Church, the Crown or their royal pals. Richly endowed with natural resources and sparse population, North America provided a welcome outlet for Europe's rising population pressures. The same feudal system prevailed in Japan and Korea, except those nations got a late start on colonization (or in the case of Korea, being colonized), and thus had little means for exporting a population under pressure.

So both Europe and the modernizing Asian countries turned to government-supported development and protection of their industries. And, in the 20th century, instead of exporting population, Europe and Asia increasingly produced and exported goods. After World War II, U.S. policy strongly supported democracy and free enterprise in the Axis states of Germany and Japan. At home, domestic rules encouraged imports while discouraging the export of American industrial (but not agricultural) output. To a considerable extent, one could argue that Detroit became an unwitting victim of the Cold War, in which it was more important for American interests to support manufacturing in Europe and Japan (and later Korea) to strengthen those countries against the threat of Soviet domination than to support our own, homegrown industries.

Many people have forgotten that the first foreign automobile company to make inroads in the U.S. (and other export markets) was Volkswagen of Germany in 1949. After the war, VW was up for grabs, but the U.S. automakers passed. VW thus became owned by a combination of state and federal German government entities. That same government ownership—direct or indirect—was true of automobile companies in France and Italy. Of course, those governments actively discouraged the import of American vehicles, the reason being that in the years right after World War II, there was a huge balance of payments problem; the bankrupt countries of Europe did not want to spend their precious hordes of American dollars on American goods while needing to build up their own industrial employment. However, at least in Germany, General Motors and Ford were allowed to operate their pre-war Continental subsidiaries reasonably unfettered. Ironically, in recent years European auto plants have had to hire imported laborers from the Mediterranean, Middle East and Africa.

Nevertheless, it is clear European countries have enjoyed national industrial policies friendly to manufacturing while at the same time creating sanctuary markets.

An entirely different situation evolved in Japan and Korea. Under the industrial policy for Japan established by the "American Caesar," General Douglas MacArthur, American auto companies were simply prohibited from re-opening their pre-war plants that had been confiscated by the Japanese government or to own more than a minority interest in Japanese companies. Japan has relatively little land area to support its population agriculturally. A combination of government and banking combined to create what has been described as "Japan Incorporated" for support of manufacturing to export. In addition, unlike North America and Europe, Japan has a homogenous population with an exceedingly strong nationalistic and exclusionary culture dating back centuries. Japan today is the world's third largest national auto market, from which foreign cars are largely excluded. Again, these factors create a sanctuary market for Japanese companies in Japan. That's not to say U.S. automakers haven't established technical and investment ties with Japanese automakers. Ford linked with Mazda, GM with Isuzu and Suzuki, and Chrysler with Mitsubishi. But while the U.S. has remained wide open for automotive imports from Japan and transplant factories in the U.S., there's no vice versa.

The situation with Korea is somewhat the same, except that free, democratic and entrepreneurial South Korea would have been overrun by Communist North Korea except for intervention from the United Nations—primarily U.S. and British/Australian forces. Like Japan, Korea had an historical feudal land system, compounded by Chinese and Japanese colonization. Like the Japanese, Koreans are intensely nationalistic. Also like Japan, Korea has a national industrial policy to encourage manufacturing and export, to the exclusion of foreign goods. The Korean auto industry has grown hugely in recent years, largely for export but also to supply the growing domestic market resulting from national prosperity. Again, except for GM's current position in Daewoo and Ford's former part-ownership of Kia, for all practical purposes American automakers have been excluded from Korea, creating yet another sanctuary market.

The bottom line is that the U.S. needs a national industrial policy that supports blue-collar and white-collar workers and their employers as well as farmers. (See page 29.)

Populist Anti-Business Bias

The second external factor affecting Detroit is the century-long bias against business. Anti-business bias in the U.S. dates to the opening of the 20th century and populist attacks, however justified, against Big Steel, Big Oil, Big Meat Packing, and others, resulting in a flurry of anti-trust laws and the over-regulation of interstate commerce. This bias pretty much went underground during the prosperous Roaring Twenties, despite the influx of European Socialists and a few Communists, but came back with passion in the Great Depression. Labor organizers found it handy to demonize business, and politicians found it was a good vote-getter. During the New Deal, auto executives were hauled before congressional committees for haranguing, long before the onset of television. To be sure, there always has been a strong populist strain among

Americans who, for the most part were rebellious even before arriving on North American shores in whatever century.

More than 50 years ago, Washington's bias against the auto industry—and the willingness of the media and activist groups to misrepresent—was amply demonstrated in the deliberate and continued misquotation of General Motors' former President and Secretary of Defense Charles E. Wilson, who testified before Congress that, "What is good for the country is good for General Motors." The testimony was misquoted to arrogantly claim: "What is good for General Motors is good for the country." GM produced transcripts of the testimony to no avail; the slur on Wilson and GM continued for years. It became one of the longest lasting of all urban myths. The other long-lasting myth concerning GM was that the country's largest industrial enterprise had conspired to force streetcar companies into bankruptcy. To the contrary, millions of the public voted with their feet—buying automobiles to free themselves from the tyranny of public transportation systems and the not-infrequent strikes that shut them down.

A couple of years after the misquotation incident, a book entitled *The Insolent Chariots*, an elitist critique of Detroit styling and annual model changes, was published to much Boston–New York–Washington acclaim. It became pretty clear that in addition to the elitist versus blue-collar autoworker schism, there was the cultural/geographic split between the two coasts and the heartland.

And there was no let-up in vigorous anti-trust action against Detroit during this period. In the late 1950s and early 1960s, Detroit was filled with rumors that the Justice Department would compel General Motors to divest Chevrolet. This never came to pass, but Justice did force Ford to divest its purchase of the Electric Auto-Light company's automotive battery and spark-plug business, despite the fact that arch-competitor GM had owned such operations for decades.

The 1960s saw the growth of anti-automobile activist groups in Washington and California, the former focused on automotive safety and the latter on alleged pollutants. Their power and consequent successes were marked by passage of federal automotive safety regulations applied to cars, as well as national vehicle and factory emissions regulations. California led the pack, chasing all but one automotive assembly plant out of the state—there were nine at one time—but could do nothing to curb massive population immigration. Their need for new energy and vehicles more than offset any gains from suppressing plant and vehicle pollutants. This was compounded by the insurance industry gaining en-actment of so-called "bumper laws," largely to inflate their own profits. While all these new regulations ultimately produced measurable ben-efits to the public, they were promulgated with no consideration of the economic impact on the automobile industry because of compressed timing. A national industrial policy would have provided more rational approaches to the emotionally driven laws.

The industry had not recovered from the imposition of these often im-practical and detrimental regulatory changes when it was hit by the dual whammy of the Arab Oil Embargo of 1973 and the congressionally man-dated Corporate Average Fuel Economy law of 1975. Ironically, U.S. ve-hicle regulations drove the venerable VW Beetle from the U.S. market, while at the same time allowing Japanese companies to capitalize on the American market by offering higher-mileage, 4-cylinder economy cars —Japan had no V6s or V8s at the time. To be sure, these Asian imports were well-designed and generally (but certainly not universally) high-quality cars of superior reliability. (That Detroit cars were not competi-tive on these points is a matter to be considered among several internal factors.)

Also beginning in the late 1970s, Detroit was besieged by plaintiff law-yers presenting their one-sided arguments to the media. Although im-ports were not immune from legal actions, it was difficult to utilize Japa-nese- or German-language documents and badger foreign-speaking defense witnesses before juries, so plaintiff lawyers mainly concentrated on American manufacturers. Media accounts of tort actions inevitably made American products appear inferior or unsafe, fulfilling the strategy of the plaintiff bar.

Bad turned to worse when, in the 1990s, widely publicized allegations claimed Ford and GMs' European subsidiaries conspired with Nazi officials and used slave labor before and during World War II. Ford hired Yale and Harvard professor Lawrence Dowler to examine its historical records for any evidence of complicity. No such evidence was ever uncovered, yet the media treated the exoneration as un-newsworthy.

Part of this continuing anti-Detroit rhetoric is a result of a "hate America" streak among some cultural elite intellectuals, or possibly just product snobbery reflecting the coastal tilt of the elites—"If it's imported, it's got to be better; besides we wouldn't want the commoners to enjoy such forbidden fruit." This is demonstrated by the vehicle choices of America's elite. You won't find German, Japanese, or Korean government employees driving American cars, yet District of Columbia parking lots are filled with foreign makes. A recent report by *The Detroit News* on state-owned cars supplied to Michigan State University officials showed the three top athletic chiefs specified Lexus in their vehicle perk contracts, while the leading vehicle for University of Michigan officials was Honda, even though most U.S. Honda installations are in enemy territory—Ohio.

Given the history of the War Against the Automobile (the title of a 1977 book by Barry Bruce-Briggs), the elitist/populist bent of U.S. politics and the coastal-versus-interior geographic competition of America, it seems unlikely Detroit can do much to moderate bias unless it recovers its reputation of technological prowess and compelling styling.

Short-Term Investment Environment

It also seems unlikely the auto industry can do much to change the unfavorable structure of the investment market, in which domestic companies are held to stricter standards than import companies. Although shares of foreign automakers are traded in U.S. stock markets, their volumes are modest because of low dividend yields—especially true of Asian companies—and boards that are homogenous to their native countries.[1] On the other hand, American companies must report quarterly results under the speculative commentaries of financial analysts who may or may not know what they are talking about, but are always available to be quoted by the media. While Japanese and Korean companies can focus on long-term goals with low interest rate government loans for implementation, U.S. companies have to answer every quarter to demands for performance that are not conducive to long-term planning. Financial analysts have a built-in conflict of interest because their employers are anxious to participate in buyouts, spin-offs, and initial public offerings from the shambles of financially pressed automakers and suppliers. And, as one knowledgeable automotive insider has observed, "Everything Wall Street analysts know about cars they have learned riding in taxicabs."

---

1 In 2007, for the first time, Toyota appointed its top American executive to join the Toyota board (he soon after resigned to become a Chrysler LLC executive). When Daimler and Chrysler "merged," there was minimal American presence on the German board, and the German company held its annual meetings in Germany despite all the Americans, especially Chrysler employees and retirees, who previously had been Chrysler stockholders. Today Chrysler/FIAT is controlled and run by the Fiat management team and is targeted to soon become 51%-owned by the Italian automaker. "Fiat could own 51% of Chrysler"; Neal Boudette; *Wall Street Journal*; 5/14/09.

Operating in a Biased, Politically Correct Culture

Because of their traditional size and, at least in former times, massive employment, Detroit's automobile companies became targets of America's politically correct culture police early on, a costly and potentially highly inefficient burden on competitive operations. The director and top executive slots in foreign companies are typically filled with males of the nationality of the country where the companies are based. Even the lower ranking officials of their American subsidiaries—who rarely set policy—seldom include women and minorities. Thus foreign companies have a competitive advantage in managing strictly on a performance— or worse, a national origin—basis, rather than having to balance personnel assignments against equal opportunity employment requirements that are rigidly enforced against American companies.

Unfortunately for Detroit, there is little that it can do to change long-term cultural shifts affecting its viability except to wait out the inevitable cyclical march of history.

INTERNAL FACTORS

When it comes to the industry's internal factors, there is no shortage of suggestions about what is wrong and how to fix it.

Detroit developed its own unique cultural environment during the automobile industry's huge growth and the success of the major producers. While each company has its own subculture, there are negative characteristics that the Big Three—General Motors, Ford, and Chrysler—share, as well as, to some extent, the supplier industry.

The three major internal factors discussed below—Management Shortcomings, Organizational Shortcomings and Union Legacies—can be corrected over time, given recognition, effective action, and lasting discipline. And change is underway, driven by non-competitive structural costs and the resulting loss of market share. That's the good news. The bad news is that there's much work to be done. As the old saying goes, *the devil is in the details*, which too often are either overlooked by management or seem incapable of being altered. Let's look at some of these details.

Management Shortcomings

First, let's talk about strategic and structural breakdown. To me, the auto companies were using a structural solution to correct a spiritual problem.

- **Board Membership.** In a recent *New York Times* Sunday Business Section column, pundit Ben Stein observed that the boards of many of the Wall Street firms suffering mortgage meltdown financial distress were filled with inexperienced directors, unable to see the danger signs or cope with them once they became apparent. The same could be said for Detroit's two remaining publicly owned automakers, Ford and General Motors. Until about 30 years ago, board seats were held by veterans of the business: either insider corporate executives, top executives from other companies, or savvy Wall Street counselors. Since the 1980s, however, GM's board has had only one inside director, locking out top engineering and other executives who in the past made major contributions. Under pressure from critics claiming to represent both public interest and equal-opportunity forces, in the last three decades all major corporate boards have come under fire for lack of diversity. Companies generally responded by retiring experienced directors to be replaced with inexperienced advocates. Robert Winters, retired head of Prudential, laments that current directors have only two responsibilities: loyalty to the enterprise and diligence in protecting stockholder interests. Whether this kind of loyalty has always been required by automotive boards is debatable, but surely an inexperienced or weak board is more likely to rubber-stamp management proposals rather than call for studies for better understanding.[2]

- **Management by Ego.** The halls of Detroit are filled with tales of disastrous policies or programs pursued by a new top executives simply "to make his mark" on the organization or its products. Admittedly, these moves on occasion became hits, but more often they turned out to be disasters. At Ford, this phenomenon came to be known as the "cult of the personality," and was described as an outgrowth of the ego-driven character of Western European and American males to win for themselves rather the team or the institution. Asians culturally are more attuned to teamwork and the good of the company and their country.

- **Executive and Management Turnover.** Like the military, the auto industry has long had human development policies that dictated moving personnel every two to three years, often to different cities, as a means of promotion and training. Although moving around appeals to some, the policy is disruptive to family life and all too often produces inefficiency while discouraging the development of deep, in-place knowledge and expertise. At Toyota for example, the top engineer on a given vehicle line typically remains in that job for nine to ten years. U.S. personnel systems traditionally have lacked the means to reward promising talent while keeping them in place. Rapid turnover conspires to threaten quality, long-range planning and consistency of execution, and surely is a factor in failed marketing.

---

2 Critics have also charged that boards with inside directors are also prone to rubber-stamping management proposals, because of all the "yes men." (See pages 41-42 and 200-201.)

- **Inability to Create and Execute Long-Range Plans.** Short-range planning is an inevitable result of quarterly financial reporting disciplines, as well as the constant turnover of management personnel, inexperienced boards, and finance-driven internal goals, but establishing and executing long-term strategic plans has been a major management shortcoming of Detroit-trained executives. However, with two of the three new auto company CEOs from outside the industry, there's a rare opportunity to transform this shortsighted culture. At this writing, Ford CEO Alan Mulally, a former high-level Boeing executive, has made a sweeping turnaround. Chrysler and Fiat's Sergio Marchionne, the only auto guy, has also made a start in reshaping Chrysler's fortunes. GM's Dan Akerson, with a background in telecommunications and less than a year as CEO, remains a question mark.

- **Excessive Influence of Finance Staffs.** The Harvard Business School teaches that businesses go through three cycles: beginnings, when they are run by inventors, engineers, or entrepreneurs; growth, when they are driven by production experts; and decline, when they are unduly influenced by accountants. General Motors built its long-lasting but now threatened dominance of the modern automobile industry with its combination of styling, product development, marketing mastery, and financial controls. Ford regained its strength after World War II through the disciplines introduced by financial and logistics experts recruited from the Army Air Corps, General Motors, and university campuses. This time of growth has passed. Too many bad decisions have been governed by shortsighted financial policies, the most notorious and harmful probably being customer-alienating warranty administration, closely followed by product-feature strangulation driven by needed, but often market-contrary, budgetary concerns.

- **Alienation from Dealers and the Retail Market.** It's an old joke in the auto industry that very few high-ranking corporate executives have been able to make the transition to being successful retail deal-ers. Indeed, the curse of the business—domestic or import—is the alienation of company people from dealers and retail customers. Company people drive Company Cars, serviced at Company garag-es. A purchase negotiation is unknown. But more critically, drivers of company cars do not have to face the problems a retail customer has with product deficiencies—not only the haggling and uncertain-ties of being dealt with fairly and the costs, but the challenges of finding substitute transportation, not to mention the inconvenient service hours working people face. It is hard to take away long-ac-cepted perks such as company cars, but forcing their delivery and servicing through retail establishments might go a long way to im-prove customer relations and the reputation of Detroit. Actually, lon-ger warranties, road service, and other customer-friendly marketing programs have been steps in the right direction, but almost too little and too late for Detroit's eroding market share.

- **Poor marketing.** Lack of customer focus is foremost among mar-keting goofs of the last several decades. Others include abandon-ing established brand names, abandoning loyal customers, chasing fads, awkward introductions (announcing a new product too long before its on-sale date), and unimaginative copycat products. Then there's the consistent, year-after-year offering of dull and stodgy styling. It's hard to tell one make of mid-sized sedan from another. With the exception of the Ford Mustang, none have the "gotta have," "gotta see" sex appeal that draws new customers to dealerships.

Organizational Shortcomings

- **Parts and Service.** The most obvious organizational shortcoming of the automobile industry is the inherent conflict created by combining Parts and Service under one umbrella, an arrangement that has become an industry standard. Ultimately, the goal of successful customer relations rests upon minimal service, and when service is necessary, good performance. What has happened, however, is that P & S organizations have become a vehicle for pushing parts sales and their profits. Service is a treated by Finance as a costly burden. To give credit where due, around 1970 Ford tried to separate the two functions with the creation of a Customer Service Division, but it was squeezed out at the first threat of declining corporate products. How different the company's product reputation would have been had the Service Division been allowed to live, assuming Service would have had the internal power to drive engineering and manufacturing to design and build sounder products.

  Further, because Finance has no way of measuring the future, warranty administration is driven by budgets rather than by customer loyalty. Even in this day of computerized records, U.S. companies have no ready mechanism other than parts sales to track out-of-warranty performance. Hence, import companies have legitimately come to be known for longer lasting, more reliable products. Should there be an organization devoted to long-range planning, pinned to out-of-warranty performance and customer loyalty of five years or more? Absolutely!

- **Quality Control.** A second major internal organizational shortcoming has been Detroit manufacturer's reluctance to take on Asian-level quality control, which then required decades of retraining and catching up. To be sure, external measurements of GM and Ford products in North America now show them equal or superior to the best importers have to offer—but it took a quarter of a century, with many slips in between, to reach those levels. Was that a correctible organizational problem or a cultural block? We may never know, and indeed it is fair to observe that not all Japanese auto companies are created equal when it comes to quality.

Union Legacies

It has been fashionable among elitist critics not associated with the left side of the spectrum or with Big Labor to blame Detroit's problems on lazy, greedy, or inept workers, from the shop floor to the executive suite. Others point the finger at Big Labor itself, especially the United Auto Workers and other industrial unions representing rubber, steel, and electrical workers.

• **The United Auto Workers.** In the case of the UAW, the charge is that labor agreements forced on manufacturers made them non-competitive with import companies. The elements of excessive cost include (1) healthcare, since Asian and European industrial countries have government-subsidized medical coverage and employees of "transplant" factories in the U. S. are younger and healthier than those of "old" Detroit; (2) pensions and related retirement costs, again since importers benefit from state-supported retirement benefits and "transplant" employees and, as with health care, they have not yet reached retirement age; (3) the cost of tighter controls in hiring, paying, and assigning workers than in competitors' newer, non-union transplant facilities; and (4), the indirect cost American companies face in paying for union representatives in their plants.

   But union officials are between a rock and a hard place. Unlike company officials and critics, union chiefs are elected by their members through democratic procedures. To be re-elected and re-main effective, leaders must answer to their members' demands, however impractical, costly, or merely politics-as-usual. Moreover, union leaders find themselves in the awkward position of having to "sell" to their members new labor agreements which contain "give-backs" of reduced wages, benefits, or work rules, thus minimizing the host company from losses due to import company cost advantages. Only time and the realities of closing domestic auto plants due to lost market share can force new thinking on America's union members. The unions themselves are reacting by signing on government white-collar employees to replace blue-collar factory workers in their membership.

- **Globalization.** In the auto industry, the real issue—with both management and the UAW—is the failure to recognize, decades ago, the threat of global economic forces, in which a national industrial policy might have provided relief. As explained above, the U.S. helped Asian and European nations develop such policies as a defense against Soviet threats during the Cold War.

- **Work Ethic.** It is believed that UAW leadership also tolerated poor work ethic, tolerance of gross misconduct, and illegal activities such as drug trade and gambling. Also, for decades it was considered fair game for the union to torment the companies on every level. The most blatant UAW demand, which it won in strike-or-concede bargaining, was the creation of the so-called "jobs bank" that paid laid-off workers for not working.[3]

The internal problems in the domestic auto industry are capable of being overcome by recognition, understanding, will, and perseverance. That's a tall order and will test the American "can do" ethic. But as they say, where there's a will there's a way.

In the next chapter, **The Black Swan**, we'll look at how Ford, General Motors and all of American industry could be facing the full force of the first

---

3 Like numerous other UAW concessions made in the lead-up to the 2008 government bailout at GM and Chrysler, job banks were abolished.

depression of the 21st century. The last two of the true, American auto manufactures could become completely overwhelmed with debt just like some of their automotive predecessors who went out of business during the last Great Depression.

THE BLACK SWAN

We are not afraid to entrust the American people with unpleasant facts, foreign ideas, alien philosophies, and competitive values. For a nation that is afraid to let its people judge the truth and falsehood in an open market is a nation that is afraid of its people. —John F. Kennedy, 35th U.S. president (1917-1963)

On September 20, 2010, The National Bureau of Economic Research (NBER) declared that the longest recession since the Great Depression officially ended in June, 2009. That was the same month General Motors declared bankruptcy.

I am a positive upbeat person. All through my life, I have always tried to find the bright side of the situation. But, I believe that this nation could have a second dip in the economy in 2012, and one far more worse than the drop in 2008 because the major product produced in the United States is debt. It was the banking industry's horrific debt in 2008; it will be U.S. government's rising debt in 2011 and 2012 that could start the downward trend and The Next Great Depression.

THE NATIONAL DEBT

It seems like almost everyone in the United States has been living like there is no tomorrow. Debt has been accruing over many years and most have over-borrowed. Whether it be personal, business, city, state, or national government—everyone is almost overwhelmingly overextended.

The national debt has increased an average of $4.10 billion per day since September 28, 2007. The estimated population of the United States is 309,781,956, so each citizen's share of this debt is $45,318.76, and this number is going up at the rate of almost $5,000 a year. Consider it from my personal perspective: in the four years that I've been writing this book, the debt has increased $4,879,000,000,000.00. By the end of this year, it could go up another $1.496 trillion, perhaps more.

The World Clock even puts the situation into a better perspective.
www.poodwaddle.com/worldclock.swf

The United Stated is adding billions of dollars to the national debt daily and the clock keeps ticking. If a person ran the family budget the way Congress runs up the national debt, the bank would be forcing foreclosure.

The Ponzi Scheme

From my point of view, the United States Congress is running a gigantic Ponzi scheme: money borrowed today is going to pay interest on previous loans. Take Social Security funds for an example. The federal government has been playing around with them for some time by placing them into the General Fund to gain additional congressional revenue. These misappropriated Social Security funds amount to many of billions and billions of dollars since 1962. Today's outgoing payments are being made from Social Security incoming funds. And now the U.S. Congress wants to up the age of people retiring to reduce pay-outs. Of course, in that process they also increase the amount of money going into the country's General Fund. Members of Congress think this borrowing can go on forever, or at least not collapse on their watch. They are so wrong!

Bernard Madoff was a piker: he only dealt in BILLIONS and they put him in jail for 150 years. Too bad we can't put members of Congress in jail for misappropriating our Social Security funds!

Worst of all, the expanding national debt and printing QE3 will become some of the major issues that help trigger the Black Swan Event.

What's a Black Swan Event?

A Black Swan is an event with the following three attributes:

- First, it is an outlier, meaning that it lies outside the realm of regular expectations because nothing in the past can convincingly point to its possibility.

- Second, it carries an extreme impact.

- And third, in spite of its outlier status, human nature makes us concoct explanations for its occurrence after the fact, rendering it explainable and predictable.

It has been reported that many business cycles could dive for the bottom of the trough starting in late 2011. The national debt is at the root of the problem, which was reinforced on April 20, 2011, when Standard & Poors (S&P) downgraded the U.S. debt to "negative" for 2012. Worryingly, China is considering cutting back on loans to the United States, putting America in a credit squeeze and further devaluating the dollar.

The downgrade and devaluation could then pick up speed as U.S. Treasury officials strive to increase the stated 2011 debt ceiling to over $1.5 trillion, not the $1.2 trillion originally projected by the Obama Adminis-

It is estimated that there may be as many as a trillion U.S. World Currency Dollars in circulation, floating around the world.

tration. This could cause a hyper-inflationary situation because the risk to investors is becoming monumental in U.S. government paper. Our government is printing fiat money! The value of the U.S. dollar could soon become almost worthless. If the senseless printing of money continues, the price of gasoline and gold will just keep rising.

When a country's currency becomes practically worthless, the economy goes to hell in a hand basket. Also, as the dollar devaluates, it could be dethroned as the World Reserve Currency, thus dropping its value even further. Every person around the world who has U.S. dollars in their possession will want to divest those dollars immediately. When that happens, the U.S. dollar could go into a vertical downward slide in value. Every living person in the United States will lose massive asset value overnight.

In the end, the economic collapse of the United State will be very similar to that of the Soviet Union. The United States will run out of money just like the Soviet Union did in 1991, wildly competing for armament during the Cold War.

But there's more. Along with the crisis outlined above, the following situations could also have a major affect in causing the Black Swan Event:

- Total unrest in the Middle East, as financially poor people rise to power and overthrow ruling royal families. The overthrow of the Saudi ruling royal family will cause a domino effect of loss of U.S. influence in Saudi Arabia and other oil producing nations. Egypt, Iran, and Yemen can totally disrupt over 60% of the world's oil distribution because they control the oil distribution's choke points. The price of oil and the distribution structure that we know will be greatly changed.

- The collapse of the European Market as it was originally structured, The euro as a monetary unit will cease to exist as more and more Euro nations become insolvent.

- Many municipal bonds will collapse as major U.S. cities, county, and state governments default on their financial obligations. Many funded pension plans will only be able to pay a subsistence monthly retirement check, which will have a dramatic effect on the overall U.S. economy. Currently city, state and national economies are all counting on the over 60,000,000 retirees spending their retirement money.

- A large-scale uprising of the lower income masses in China could be the wild card that triggers a Black Swan Event single-handedly. The economic boom has passed them over, and the communist dictatorship will be hard pressed to stop a mass uprising because the whole world will be watching. Many thought the overthrow of an Arabic dictatorship was next to impossible, and soon they were falling like dominoes. Nowadays anything can happen!

SURVIVE AND PROSPER

The intentions of this book are not to scare people, but to point out what can be done in order for the U.S. to survive and prosper as an industrial nation. The main question is, *Are we still an industrial nation?*

American citizens are becoming concerned about the deindustrialization of America. Many people feel that the United States will become the first post World War II industrialized nation to lose its industrial base.

Without industry, the United States becomes a nation with so much debt it will collapse and cease to function even as a second-rate nation. The perception is the Chinese possibly may soon own, and therefore take control over this country, and that may become a reality sooner than anyone thinks. The only thing that could slow down or stop China's economic gain in power would be an uprising of the lower income mass of Chinese people. The unthinkable has already happened against dictators in the Middle East, and there is no reason it can't also happen against a communist dictatorship.

But why is the deindustrialization of America occurring? In simplistic terms, because most people in the national government have never worked in a production business operation. They have never created anything from raw materials. They do not understand manufacturing products or free trade. On the whole most government people view themselves as elitists. Elitists don't work, they just talk.

The thought process of past government officials was that the new Internet and American innovation alone would keep America in front of the competition. They were so wrong: the Internet jobs went to India. And American innovation is being left in the dust. For the record, China is graduating seven to eight engineers or scientists to every one American. I would like to think Americans are smart, but a ten to one ratio—that's a continual upstream process. I personally do not think that every American engineer can outthink seven to ten Chinese engineers. If government officials think Americans are that smart, then they are just plain STUPID.

Going on, most of the bureaucrats and elected government officials come from the service industry. They think just like the New York Stock Exchange (NYSE). In reality, the NYSE creates nothing but perception: it handles accounting transactions, charges a percentage fee for keeping tabs on the money that passes through their hands, and calls it business.

In the past, "Globalized Production" was a politically correct way of saying "I want cheap labor, the hell with America, I only care about me." Sam Walton did it at Walmart, and it has worked perfectly well. Walk in any Walmart and try to find an American manufactured product other than food? I haven't been successful in the search there. In the end, Walmart could have been one of the leaders in the deindustrialization of America.

Maybe Walmart could add a new department for just American manufactured products!

It's time to bring American nationalism back into the equation for the salvation of the United States!

Let's Talk About Salvation

Since the inception of the American Auto Industry in the early 1900s, more than 60 automobile manufactures have been in a constant struggle of consolidating into the remaining Detroit Big Three. What's left has been functioning on very short margins for a long time without any government support and a depression will cause an almost total collapse of the industry we know today. In 2012 and beyond, it could be very difficult for what's left of the American Auto Industry to compete against foreign companies in Germany and Japan, Korean, and China (the Asian

Tigers) that are provided financial support by the banking and government agencies in their respective countries.

But I'm not just talking about the salvation of the American Auto Industry; **I'm talking about the salvation of the United States as an industrialized nation as a whole.**

The United States is probably the only industrialized nation without a working industrial policy. American companies have shipped jobs overseas to reduce costs under a restructuring process called "globalization," and by doing so these companies are now global organizations. If the only opportunity for employment for the entire working class of the United States is in the service sector, there will soon be few people with enough income to purchase new vehicles. The U.S. could be reduced to the status of a Banana Republic Nation well before the middle half of the 21st century.

In the end, the United States cannot continue to purchase foreign goods as a debtor nation whose major manufacturing product is printing billions of U.S. dollars each year with no thought of the consequences. For all of the good intentions of the U.S. government, the continual debt increase of over $1 trillion each year will be our downfall and one of the prime initiators of the First Depression of the 21st century.

Yes, the situation is that bad, but legislatures on the federal, state, and local level are all acting like ostriches with their heads in the sand. The reality of the situation appears that no one knows what to do, so nothing is being done.

The nation could go into a depression in 2012 without anyone in government understanding what can or has to be done about it. It is the goal of Look Out America to outline some courses of action that can be taken to avoid a financial catastrophe. It is better to take a look at these options now than assume the ostrich position and let the United States collapse into a debtor nation status.

THE U.S. NEEDS A STRATEGIC PLAN

The reason most people never reach their goals is that they don't define them, or ever seriously consider them as believable or achievable. Winners can tell you where they are going, what they plan to do along the way, and who will be sharing the adventure with them. —Denis Waitley

THE SYSTEM IS BROKEN

The United States as a nation is on the verge of collapse, along with many state and local governments. To be realistic the entire U.S. system is broken

> **Financially**
> **Economically**
> **in Energy Policy**
> **and Infrastructure**

It is broken

> **Morally**
> **in Industrial Policy**
> **and Government Services**
> **and Education**

... just to name a few.

The United States as a nation is the greatest user of energy per citizen in the world, but does not have a good National Energy Policy or Strategic Plan. With increasing oil prices, oil will become a larger portion of the United States trade imbalance. The Department of Energy (DOE) does not control energy policy effectively.

On average, the United States is borrowing over $4 billion a day without any plan on how to pay that debt back. There is no Strategic Repayment Plan. United States is currently paying over 41.8% of the money borrowed each day as interest. In the past, economists established 40% as the tipping point where a hyperinflation disaster could start to occur. If hyperinflation sets in, the United States could look like pre-revolutionary America, where it took many, many Continental dollars just to buy a loaf of bread. Eventually, the Continental dollar became valueless. Theoretically, this could happen again.

The U.S. government has monetized an even larger portion of the national debt by the printing of 1.6 trillion additional dollars as a Quantitative Easing (QE1 and QE2). Now QE3 is being considered as the next round of placating the situation.

U.S. students rank very low in relation to other nations when it comes to education, but the United Stated does not have a clear-cut Educational Policy or Strategic Plan. Other nations apparently do. It is about time Washington bureaucrats realize that the future of the United States lies in hands of well-educated grandchildren.

Only the U.S. Military has a Strategic Plan. And the only place the United States shines in Strategic Planning is in the Military. The U.S. is the only super power in the world at this time, but at this writing, China is working toward building up a technical military advantage that is fully capable of challenging the U.S.

**What Does the United States Have to Do to Become
Successful Again?**

It is industry that creates products from raw materials that add the greatest value to the economic growth of a nation. The United States is still listed as one of the worlds' industrialized nations, but the U.S. does not have an Industrial Policy or an Industrial Strategic Plan that is working. It is about time for the United States to start looking at role models if it wants to improve the business climate and the job situation. We need a National Strategic Plan that focuses on saving the United States' industrial base, with focused guidelines of integrating both labor and manufacturing into one cohesive goal of restructuring to produce goods and products on American soil, if for nothing else but U.S. consumption.

WHAT'S A STRATEGIC PLAN?

Most governmental officials in Washington, even most businessmen, do not have an inkling of what makes up a Strategic Plan.

A Strategic Plan is written statement as to:

1. Philosophy of the business

2. The scope and nature of business to be pursued

3. An outlook for the future

4. Management's requirement for a business plan

5. Geographical limitations for the business, if any, and

6. Results expected

Now that you have the definition, you may want to know why we need a Strategic Plan? Here's why:

- A Strategic Plan is a road map to guide the nation (or a business) into the future. It highlights the ever-changing terrain (conditions) that is always part of any future.

- A Strategic Plan also provides guidelines for good governance.

- The structural guidelines of a Strategic Plan understand both the Best-Case Scenario and Worst-Case Scenario. By considering both the good and the bad, prudent and wise choices can be made so that the situation doesn't get ugly when under pressure in the marketplace.

- Finally, a Strategic Plan helps nations and businesses avoid problems, gain ground on competitors, maximize profits, listen to good ideas, and be good world citizens.

The U.S. Strategic Plan needs to focus on the following:

- **Pride.** Instill pride in the government of the United States of America. Pride will return with the government's all-out focus on industrial development. We need to develop industry as if we were at war! For we are at war: the United States is being carved up and being sold off as if we had lost World War II. Yes, we are talking about an all-out war. We are trying to save the United States of America from collapse and takeover by China.

- **Immigration.** Strengthen U.S. borders to eliminate unlawful entry. Legal immigrants make better lawful citizens. Entering the U.S. illegally is their first unlawful act, making them criminals in American society. This country was made great because it was the melting pot of nations. Legal immigrants from all over the world are the backbone of the United States, not illegal immigrants by the millions, trying to escape poverty in their own countries.

- **Education.** Develop an educational system that once again becomes the best in the world. The current K–12 system is out of touch given the fast pace of the today's the digital age. Provide U.S. students with .02% student loans. And no financial aid for Eligible Non-Citizen status.

- **Morality.** The United States must live within its financial means at the national, state and city levels.

- **Priorities.** The United States should stop being the savior of the world. It is time we focus on saving ourselves, and let someone else save the world. Plus, the United States can no longer buy friendship and prop up dictators with billions of U.S. dollars.

- **Invest.** Support healthy savings rates as an indicator of financial stability. With savings, investments increase, along with innovation, increased productivity, and a growth in employment.

- **More Pride.** Put pride back into being an American citizen. Incite citizens to look toward to the future with a new sense of frugality. As a nation, we should pay off our debts and thereby ensure the success of our children and grandchildren. The nation's problems should not be passed on to the next generation. As a nation, we should emulate the national bird, the Bald Eagle, coming back from devastation to full strength in the span of one human generation. One generation should be the national timeframe for us to be debt-free.

- **Service.** Make every elegible U.S. citizen serve in the military to understand the value of nationalism and service to country. If their children are involved, then maybe Congress won't be so ready to go to war.

Next, we need a 2012 Marshall Plan to save what's left of the United States.

INDUSTRIAL INFRASTRUCTURE

DoIT. This book proposes a new cabinet position, the Department of Industry and Technology (DoIT), just like there is a Department of Commerce and a Department of Agriculture. The United States needs a Secretary of Industry and Technology if the nation is to forge on as an industrialized nation for another 100 years.

Research. Today the Department of Defense (DoD) is spending billions of dollars on technical research at leading universities across the U.S. None of that technology is focused on or channeled into the industrial community because the Department of Defense considers their research highly confidential. Yet many of the people doing the research at the leading universities are foreign nationals working on their PhD. programs. When they graduate, they return to government posts in their own countries to continue research for their own militaries and industrial communities with the knowledge gained at the United States military's expense. Why not incorporate all military research under the DoIT Program? In the future, I envision that DoD funds will only be channeled to American students in our leading universities. Some of that research money and technology must be diverted to give American industrial corporations a technical edge, so that the vast amount of monies spent on military research will at least have some practical use in the real world.

This way, the American public will be getting a technical advantage from their tax dollars.

Business Access Fee. We must create an environment where enterprising entrepreneurs can flourish, and I propose support for a Business Access Fee for companies to enter and exploit the lucrative American markets. This is similar what President Theodore Roosevelt was talking about when he said that tariffs "must never be reduced below the point that will cover the difference between the labor cost here and abroad. The well-being of the wage worker is a prime consideration of our entire policy of economic legislation."[1] That bit of information has certainly been lost in Washington. D.C.—on the bureaucrats and policymakers, anyway, who are cozy with lobbyists.

A protective tariff in the form of a "Business Access Fee" should be placed on imports from cheaper labor countries whose workers compete for the same jobs as Americans do. The playing field has to become level, and in the past the United States government has always tilted in favor of foreign competition. If Walmart had to pay a Business Access Fee to cover the difference between the labor cost here and abroad for manufactured goods, it probably would not have half the number of stores they have today.

Lee Iacocca has been saying for years that the playing field was tilted in favor of foreign manufactures. Nothing will ever change until lobbyists are banned from Washington and politicians start thinking about the salvation of America, rather than their own personal salvation.

Jobs. Employment can be stimulated through the combined efforts of industry, universities, and the U.S. government, all focused on developing technology that produce jobs. We should look to the nations that are flooding our markets now with products that sap jobs from the American workers.

---

1 From the article in the WorldNetDaily; "Lower wages is not a sound national strategy"; Roger Simmermaker; 12/13/10.

If the U.S. were to close over half its bases overseas and furlough U.S. servicemen, the unemployment rate would soar to 1932–1933 levels of 24%. The only alternative would be to redeploy military personnel to protect the U.S. southern borders.

At the present time, the real unemployment numbers for U.S. citizens are understated at less than 10%, and they are much higher than that for U.S. military veterans returning from combat service. Government numbers are not to be trusted because they are rigged. Just like the government is saying there is no inflation because both food and fuel costs are not included. If they were included, the Social Security checks would have to be increased! So much for honest politicians.

As a nation it is about time to create a co-adhesive environment between industry, education (universities), and the government to initiate the Industrialization of America. As a nation, we need to stop the deindustrialization of America!

CONSOLIDATION AND A STRATEGIC PLAN FOR THE AMERICAN AUTO INDUSTRY

Every morning in Africa, a gazelle wakes up. It knows it must run faster than the fastest lion or it will be killed. Every morning a lion wakes up. It knows it must outrun the slowest gazelle or it will starve to death. When the sun comes up, you better start running. —Christopher McDougall

There are numerous ironies in the downward spiral of the U.S. auto industry, but at least three stand out:

- Management's failure to grasp the full implications of increasing globalization despite long overseas experience themselves.

- Its lack of technical and design prowess since the 1970s, although design and technical skill are the historical cornerstones of their success.

- Its inability to solve its adversarial relationship with the United Autoworkers union, even though both parties need each other more than ever.

WHAT DOES THE AMERICAN AUTO INDUSTRY HAVE TO DO TO BECOME SUCCESSFUL AGAIN?

Beginning in this chapter, and continuing through the end of the book, I will address these ironies, plus outline a plan to secure the survival of the American Auto Industry during the coming Black Swan Event, and ensure its success for a long time to come.

The Detroit Auto Industry is a microcosm of the national picture. Change is happening at faster pace than ever before in history of mankind. The amount of technical Information doubles every two years, and we are now living in exponential times. The new American Auto Industry of Ford and General Motors can either use the combined engineering and manufacturing efforts to forge a Strategic Plan that will keep them at pace with the rapidly changing technical conditions, or they can collapse and go out of business. It could be as simple as that.

The nation needed the industrial might of the auto industry in World War II, and Detroit was referred to as the "Arsenal of Defense." Today most of the American auto industry area of manufacturing are now idled and in decay, and the upper Midwest is now called the "Rust Belt."

If the executives of Ford and General Motors do not understand the ramifications The Next Great Depression will have on the American Auto Industry, they will go the way of many of the auto manufactures of the 1930s. Today all of Detroit's Big Three are still deeply in debt, with GM and Chrysler/Fiat shrugging off a major portion of their financial responsibility through bankruptcy. All three have thin cash reserves, and Ford still has a great amount of debt that will be very difficult to repay if the total U.S. auto market shrinks below 6,500,000 units annually, and Ford and GM combined production drops below 3,000,000 units annually.

STRATEGIC PLANNING

Theoretically, all of the Detroit Big Three have Strategic Planning departments. And over the last 40 years, each of the Detroit Big Three has made numerous changes to improve their bottom-line. In the process of making those changes, however, Ford, General Motors, and Chrysler have actually been moving backward—I know this is an oxymoron, but it's the truth. The Big Three combined have lost hundreds of billions of dollars and over 50% of market share to foreign competitors.

In reality, very few CEOs must have relied on Strategic Planning information for direction. It is hard to believe that the Detroit Big Three could lose over 50% of the automobile market in 40 years with a Strategic Plan. Top executives—plus their boards—must have felt that executive gut instinct was paramount to a plan, otherwise they would not have risen to the top of the organization. The truth is, sometimes executive egos create a world all their own. If they had a ring like the Pope, employees would have had to kiss the ring every time they entered The Office.

But think about it:

If any of the Detroit Big Three were using a Strategic Plan and still incurred a 50% market share loss, they need new Strategic Planners.

The 50% loss just didn't happen, they had to work at it, and all the executives got raises and sometimes bonuses in the process of losing market share.

HOW DID THIS HAPPEN?

It is best to sum up the last 40 years of Strategic Planning within the United States Auto Industry to better define the situation. General Motors is being used as the example because GM was the leader in automotive sales in the 1970s.

Over the years I've had much conversation with James K. Paisley, a key person in the 1970s in GM's Strategic Planning Group. As a GM Strategic Planner, Jim felt it was his duty to give the corporation both the best-case and worst-case scenario situations. James K. Paisley was not a "yes man," he was his own man, and to the GM upper management system that was his downfall. Jim was encouraged to leave GM before Roger B. Smith became chairman of General Motors on January 1, 1981. Roger did not like Jim's projections of some worst-case scenario situations for the 1980s. Had Roger B. Smith kept Jim Paisley in Strategic Planning, he would not have made so many dumb blunders. Roger replaced Jim and hired a key Strategic Planner who told him what he wanted to hear.

In 1973, Jim Paisley said:

- General Motors is being run like a third generation shoe store.

- They inherited the business.

- They have goods on the shelf.

- They have goods going out the door.

- But, no one here has the faintest idea how the business was created and how to react.

Does that sound like most family businesses that have grown under the founder and the first generation? The problem is, that when the business is passed on to the third and fourth generation, they become passive and preoccupied with the status quo and maintaining traditional policies. In other words, after the second generation, family members are no longer focused on growing the company.

Billy Durant almost put GM into bankruptcy twice in GM's early history because of creativity and over aggressiveness, and he was removed twice.

Rick Wagoner was a GM caretaker that inherited his job by being a good-looking "yes man." Everyone that dealt with Rick liked him. Rick Wagoner put GM put into bankruptcy because of lack of creativity and not doing what had to be done. For the most part, "yes men" are politically correct but not creative people in any way, shape, or form. "Yes men" can only close business operations and do not create anything new. When it comes to innovation, they have no pulse—they are flat liners.

GM's management team was at a loss when a real crisis hit, but the same was true at both Chrysler and Ford. Almost everyone in an executive position at all three corporations had become "yes men" in order to be considered for a promotion. All of these "yes men" who inherited their jobs over the last 40 years have created absolutely NOTHING. The only thing that the Detroit Big Three "yes men" were able to do in a consistent and effective fashion was lose market share. If Detroit's Big Three had had any semblance of a Strategic Planning Team guiding the respective corporations they would have fared much better.

Lee Iacocca was no "yes man" at Ford, and he got fired publicly, by Henry the Deuce. Iacocca's leadership provided both vision and trust to Chrysler workers in the early 1980s. Many retired Chrysler retirees revere Lee today as the second coming of Christ when he provided the visionary leadership to save Chrysler. Chrysler Corp. was actually saved through a lot of hard work by everyone who worked for the company at that time. But without the visionary, trustworthy leadership that Lee Iacocca provided, that could not have been done.

Lee Iacocca would have made an excellent president of the U.S. if he would have run for the position and been elected. Lee Iacocca in the eyes so many Americans is a true leader, because he was able to guide the workers of a bankrupt company to solvency. For the last 40 years the United States has never had a president that could match Lee Iacocca's leadership.

"Yes men" is what Alex Taylor III talked about in his book *From Sixty to Zero*, and the situation used as an example was the GM management team some 20-plus years after the 1973 oil embargo. All corporate executives wanted to do was to maintain status quo, nothing more nor less. This is still mostly the situation today. The Ford Motor Company now seems more focused than under past caretakers, but all three need to be focused on the looming crisis we could soon face.

THE FIRST THING: CONSOLIDATION

There needs to be a consolidation of the American Auto Industry as they face the first depression of the 21st century or they will become a sinking vessel. The Black Swan Event prediction for a full-scale depression for 2012 is definitely an anomaly, but a situation the auto industry must be prepared for as a worst-case scenario. Remember, Black Swans Events are unpredictable events that destroy prediction models.

In 1957, the US Congress wanted to break up GM because it was too large; today the combined market share of all the Detroit auto companies is much less than what GM used to be. And all will be on the verge of total collapse in the projected depression of 2012.

In order to compete and be successful in the future, Ford and General Motors need to join forces and pool their engineering and manufacturing technologies into a single technological base. A Design, Engineering, Manufacturing, Research and Development Group that both companies may draw upon must be implemented in order to survive. Currently the independent companies have their own engineering and manufacturing research facilities with a lot of duplication of effort causing a high percentage drain on corporate profits. Combining all of Ford's and General Motor's engineering and manufacturing research into one consolidated operation is definitely a paradigm shift, and one that will require considerable flexible-thinking to implement.

The Security and Exchange Commission would have a tough time ruling against such a proposal, as the combined market share of Ford and General Motors is currently lower than 40%.

A STRATEGIC PLAN FOR THE COMBINED ENGINEERING AND MANUFACTURING GROUP OF FORD AND GM

A Strategic Plan will help the industry avoid problems, gain ground on competitors, maximize profits, listen to good ideas, and be good world citizens. It will also reduce the possibility of an overzealous corporate leader implementing disastrous decisions. This is what happened at GM when a series of leaders surrounded themselves with non-automotive and poorly-informed board members. When a 50% market share is lost, it is not good governance.

Combining engineering and manufacturing technologies will probably not be the only act of consolidation for Ford and General Motors as they enter the second decade of the 21st century, but it should be the first. The service, marketing, and recycling centers could be the next stage of consolidation. (See pages 154 and 169.)

An initial statement for the new Ford and General Motors Engineering and Manufacturing Group is as follows:

BUSINESS PHILOSOPHY.   Starting with a corporate strategy, each section of the organization shall develop a compatible strategy that promotes a cooperative and synergistic relationship with the rest of the organization. Success for individual careers will be determined based on a judgment of how well this goal is accomplished, by evaluation of performance to a business plan, and by being an overall good citizen.

SCOPE and NATURE of CORPORATE BUSINESS. Worldwide development, production, and marketing of passenger cars and trucks. Manufacturing operations shall be owned jointly by Ford and General Motors. Ford and General Motors control the business and the business plan that

Chrysler is not included because they already combined engineering and manufacturing resources with Fiat after the business take over in 2009. Chrysler's engineering and manufacturing people previously had a similar relationship for eight years with Daimler Benz of Germany. With the CEO and majority control of Chrysler in the hands of Fiat, Chrysler is now a foreign company.

is approved by the Executive Committee. Final vehicle assembly plants must be able to ship components and modules for assembly worldwide. Assembly plants must be able to assemble any Ford or GM vehicle. Assembly plants and other in-house operations, if approved, should maximize automation and be designed to operate on a 24/7 basis. Labor premiums or restraints of any kind will not be acceptable. Ford or GM shall not own any dealerships. Franchises will be negotiated and dealership's facilities must be approved by Ford or GM. Dealerships will be allowed to lease and sell only new vehicles distributed by Ford or GM. A used vehicles leasing program will be developed when the Lease/Recycle Program is established. (See the chapter on the Lease/Recycle Program on page 152.)

All Ford or GM vehicles built in foreign countries and shipped to the United States for sale are subject to pay the Business Access Fee to sell in the lucrative American market. (See page 33.)

EVOLUTION of BUSINESS. This must start with a forecast of worldwide trends influenced by global problems, standards of living, and technology related to transportation. This forecast must then be comprehended in identifying the most rewarding modifications in the scope and nature of the corporate business. Avoid large sums of money on fruitless investments such as working on fuel cells when the production of hydrogen in volume is still 20 years away. This type of development may be a demonstration of good citizenship, but when started too early it will simply result in development costs that could have been used wisely in other places.

BUSINESS PLAN. A business projection of five years for each segment of the corporation that is compatible with the Corporate Strategic Plan. Ford and General Motors will have to enact a Global Strategic Plan for the next five years and also one that encompasses projections in technology for this decade. Futurists say technology is doubling every two years. With the accelerated rate of global technological development, I feel all Corporate Strategic Plans should be reviewed every three to four months. Corporate strategies and plans have to be nimble to compete in this ever-changing world.

GEOGRAPHICAL LIMITATIONS. Develop a Global Strategy.

STRATEGIC ENERGY PLAN. Both Ford and General Motors need to establish a Strategic Energy Plan to better understand how energy supply controls work. They also need to set some dramatic, clear-cut goals to improve vehicle fuel economy and reduce greenhouse emissions. This has to be done because in the past the U.S. Congress just nips at fuel economy issues to be politically correct.

The United States government has established a mediocre fuel economy plan, the Corporate Average Fuel Economy (CAFE) Standards, calling for 34.1 mpg by 2016. That CAFE Standard was put into place as an answer to counteract the auto industry building gas guzzling SUVs. (See page 133.)

The proposed government goal of a 62 mpg CAFE standard by 2025 is at the high end of the wish list. The auto industry will come kicking and screaming to the hearings scheduled for 2012, complaining that the cost to implement fuel economy will be in the BILLIONS of dollars.

The world will be looking for both new forms and lower cost energy. Ford and GM will set the United States Energy Strategy for the transportation sector, because Congress has not been able to set any significant strategy for the last 30 years. It appears that Big Oil ran both the Executive Branch and U.S. Congress. If Ford and GM want to survive, then they will determine and set the transportation goals before the U.S. Congress steps up to the plate.

With the increase of known reserves of natural gas (CH4) found within the continental United States, more plug-in, hybrid/compressed natural gas (CNG) vehicles will be built. Both the electrical and natural gas re-quirements can be resupplied from the home on a daily basis.

Ford and General Motors will also become very environmentally friendly by using alternate fuel products such as compressed natural gas, etha-nol, and bio diesel as internal combustion engine alternate fuel sources. The plug-in electrical hybrids using CNG and ethanol blends, or bio die-sel blends, will all be favorably received by the U.S. consumer, and based on the Ford and General Motors environmental commitment.

RESULTS EXPECTED

Equivalent to or better than business plan projections approved by the Executive Committee. Thousands of Ford and General Motors employ-ees and dealers think about the business on a 24/7 basis, and they should be guided by a Strategic Plan that gets them thinking about pro-posals that are in sync with Ford and GM policies. The customers, em-ployees, dealer base, and suppliers all offer an opportunity to use ideas from everyone. This would be applying good old Yankee Ingenuity to the 21st century. (See the chapter on Yankee Ingenuity on page 137.)

PART TWO: DESIGN

QUALITY AND MANUFACTURING

STYLING

QUALITY AND MANUFACTURING

Quality control is one measure GM and Ford, as the last, two American automobile manufacturers, can implement immediately to help them survive the first depression of the 21st century.

Quality and manufacturing go hand in hand. Quality must be engineered and factored into the part at the inception of part design. To me, quality is the most important element in the design and manufacturing process.

A vehicle is composed of thousands of parts that have to fit together precisely and function for at least ten years, flawlessly, in all kinds of weather and environmental conditions. So parts have to be engineered with quality in mind.

Quality is the main reason General Motors, Ford, and Chrysler have lost so many customers to foreign competition.

To better understand the relationship between quality and manufacturing, I recommend reading **Factory Man** by James E. Harbor, with James V. Higgins. The book was released in 2009, and will provide a good insight on how quality has affected American automobile manufacturing operations for the past 60 years.

Phillip Crosby

In the mid-1980s, the GM Truck and Bus Group (GM T&B) was designated as the lead division for GM's crusade on quality. At that time, I was an executive in the GM T&B Manufacturing Engineering group— responsible for Plastic Truck Parts world-wide—

and was selected to become the GM T&B Manufacturing Engineering Quality Czar. I took the assignment as a challenge because I had already witnessed and understood many of General Motors' quality shortcomings.

Phil Crosby says: "Quality is a process like raising children. You never get done."

In 1979, Philip Crosby founded Philip Crosby Associates, Inc., with headquarters in Winter Park, Florida. Philip Crosby Associates taught management how to establish a quality culture to get things done right the first time. For over 35 years, Mr. Crosby was both an illustrious philosopher and a practitioner of quality management. He emphasized that quality was a people business. GM had purchased the services of Philip Crosby as the axis on which to pivot the new General Motors quality crusade.

My first task was to understand the Philip Crosby Quality Program training process. After attending Philip Crosby Associates, Inc. in Winter Park, I asked what companies were still using the Program after five years. Honeywell's Home Products Division in Golden Valley, Minnesota, was one of them. The VP in charge of the Division was Jerre L. Stead, who said he was a finance man brought in to shepherd the division's closure because costs were out of control. Jerre turned the division totally around by strictly focusing on quality. He would sit in a portion of every quality training session so each employee understood he cared about quality. His Monday morning meetings covered a review of the quality of product shipped during the previous week. I knew that the auto industry scheduled Monday morning meetings to Schedule Overtime for the upcoming week, not the quality of product shipped. In the past, the auto industry manufacturing operations only focused on *quantity* not *quality*. At the time of our visit, the Honeywell Home Products Division commanded a 62% share of their market due to low cost and excellent quality.

Jerre Stead was most hospitable to us during our three-day visit, and wanted us (representing GM) to see everything they were doing. The most impressive was the total reliance on statical process control. Every operation was run using a 24 Sigma Statical Quality standard. When using a 24 Sigma Statical Quality system, only 5 parts in a million need to be checked, which in their case freed up 1/4 of the 3 million square foot floor space for additional production. Honeywell called the process "pull-through manufacturing," in contrast with the traditional push-through manufacturing process, where parts are waiting to be inspected before being pushed to the next manufacturing operation.

With the 24 Sigma Statistical Quality Standard, a true part cost could be established. This coincided with my own belief that product design should be as simple as possible, and with the fewest number of parts. When a part is deleted from the design, the part becomes a cost saving. Meanwhile, the auto industry was proud of their quality achievement when the standards were up from 3 Sigma to 6 Sigma. So much for accepting a high statical quality standard.

I started off working with the support of full-time facilitators and class trainers. Every employee in Manufacturing Engineering had to attend one, three-hour Crosby Quality College Zero Defect training program for ten consecutive weeks. At the start of the new 1988 GMT 400 light pick-up truck program, about 180 pick-up boxes were all welded, then set aside because they were not up to quality specifications. I wanted the VP of the GM Truck and Bus Group to be photographed driving a forklift truck into the defective pick-up boxes to show he stood by the new quality program we were preaching. But instead of throwing the 180 pick-up boxes out, someone ordered the defective boxes to be added piece-meal to the production operation assembly line. All of the money spent for quality training was for naught, and the Crosby Quality Program became what GM employees later called, "The Program of the Month."

Over the years General Motors had many "Program of the Month" projects, and it appeared each program was supported by a group of ADD (Attention Deficit Disorder) people.

W. Edwards Demming

After the Crosby Quality Program, GM hired W. Edwards Demming, the quality guru who established Japan's Industrial Quality Program. In a few short years, Edwards Demming single-handedly turned Japan around from building poor-quality junk to high-quality VCRs, TVs, and cars. Demming went to Japan because the American manufacturing community was not listening to his message of statistical process control. But the Japanese did, and Edwards Demming is a hero in Japan. The winning of the Edwards Demming Award was the pinnacle of quality achievement for a Japanese manufacturer.

I was able to attend one of Demming's last presentations at General Motors when he was at the tender age of 90. He was spot on! Too bad so many GM executives only stayed for the first hour, then took off and returned only for lunch. After lunch, they skipped out again, but made it back for the 4:00 p.m. closing remarks. No wonder GM's quality was in such disarray in the 1990s. Very few in General Motors' management team cared or were listening.

Truth Telling

Then, on December 8, 2008, the worst of the worst happened: GM openly apologized in the news media by confessing that GM had built poor-quality vehicles in the past. They openly admitted that the corporation had cut corners on quality, all at GM customer's expense. Hollow promises followed, with the Vice Chairman telling the press that GM is putting quality back into GM vehicles. Not many people believed him. The old phrase applies: "Actions speak louder than words." It's too bad General Motors executives did not understand that **"Quality is remembered, long after price is forgotten."** If GM had been forthright in the first place and hadn't cheated their customers by cutting corners, they would not have had to file for bankruptcy in 2009. By the way, it's not like GM had the corner on the market in the production of poor-quality vehicles: both Ford and Chrysler were able to match GM's poor quality in the same time frame.

GM was able to shed a lot of its old stockholders through bankruptcy, many of whom were General Motors retirees. Even now, there is still a bit of suspicion in anything GM does because GM retirees don't trust them. That came through loud and clear from people responding to our website, **LookOutAmerica.org.**

The quickest way for the auto industry to restore their corporate image is by building the highest quality vehicles on the planet. This can be accomplished by using a 24 Sigma Statical Process Control quality audit system for every part in the vehicle. From what I have observed, a 24 Sigma Statical Process Control system actually saves money when customer satisfaction and warranty costs are factored in.

BUILDING A BETTER CAR

At this juncture, both Ford and General Motors need to move together in a totally new direction as to what type of vehicles they manufacture for profit. The truck segment that now composes over 50% of total vehicle sales will slump like in 2008. A full-size truck will no longer be affordable just for personal transportation because the cost of fuel will be in the $6 to $7 range.

All automobile manufacturers around the world are in the same dilemma and haunted by the same question: "What is the proper product direction to pursue?" There are numerous new venues to choose from, ranging from a full complement of fuels and power plant combinations: gasoline, natural gas, methanol, bio-fuels, and diesel to hybrids that can be plugged in with a variety of engine configurations to total electric vehicles powered by fuel cells. Trucks, long the "bread and butter" of U.S. automakers, will have to become much more fuel efficient, designed as hybrids and manufactured for a profit at a reduced volume.

Details of options the U.S. automakers must rigidly consider to raise fuel economy and lower pollution are found on page 133.

IT'S TIME TO FORGET ABOUT THE PAST AND MOVE ON

Only when the U.S. automakers take control of their own destiny, will change occur. Ford and General Motors are the only two, true American automotive companies left, and they are both over 100 years old. They are the last in a long line of American automotive companies playing the deadly game of the survival of the fittest. This is no time for the timid. Bold life or death innovative decisions have to be made NOW!

STYLING

When it comes an automotive sales, it's all about the Design (style), Price (value), and Quality (also value), in that order, that determines VALUE in a customer's mind. Even impulse purchases based on design must also include value to the customer. In reality, the STYLING of a vehicle is EVERYTHING to the customer at point of purchase. In fact, many people purchase more vehicle than they need or can afford based on STYLING. I know, because I've done it.

WHAT IS THE PROBLEM?

For the past 30 or more years, the majority of American vehicle designs have been lackluster in appearance. It seems that the vehicle designs were conceived with the financial department cost estimators sitting in the studio passing judgment based on low cost targets.

People who only look at the retail sticker price of a car, and nothing else, are what sales people call "bottom feeders." Very few new vehicles are sold to bottom feeders. (Bottom feeders are people with a low income and have difficulty getting credit.) The five-year-old and older used cars are typically the vehicles bottom feeder's purchase.

Continually offering customers bland and uninspiring vehicles is a sure way to go out of business. Look back at the Studebaker and Packard vehicle offerings in the early 1960s as an excellent example of what happens when you combine dull, unexciting vehicle designs with little value: both companies lost sales and went out of business. Now look at GM and Chrysler in 2009: Both filed bankruptcy because they were not selling enough vehicles to support their respective business organization. Both organizations had manufacturing capability without sales capability.

The bottom line is that customers are only interested in vehicles that have an excellent appearance that will remain in style and still have value before the vehicle wears out. Fewer people are interested in performance when gasoline is over $4 per gallon.

PERCEPTION

When people purchase a vehicle, appearance is the major factor once the price range is established. The perception of a person's status is made by the price and appearance of the vehicle they drive. Like it or not, everyone uses a preconceived status judgment mechanism when they observe a person in a vehicle. For example, a person driving a new Ferrari 599 GTB Fiorano would be perceived to be of a much higher status than someone driving a new Ford Focus or Chevrolet Cobalt. It's just human nature, and that's why the name and design of the vehicle becomes so important to the buyer when purchasing a vehicle.

When the owner of a company that supplies plastic parts to the auto industry purchased his new 2005 Rolls Royce Phantom, he was concerned that he was overstating his status. But he wanted the vehicle, and could afford it. Plus, he had a few top-of-the-line cars from the Detroit Big Three to take to business meetings so the purchasing agents would understand his profit margins were in line.

I suggested to him that a way to change the perception was to purchase a personalized license plate that said LOTTO. The State of Michigan lottery commission would love it. Think of all of the poor people who will purchase a Michigan Lottery ticket based on a Rolls Royce Phantom with a LOTTO license plate. And as Tom Peters used to say in his lectures, "Perception is Everything."

BUYERS AND THE LIFE CYCLE OF VEHICLES

When people purchase a new vehicle, they try to find something that compliments their personality and lifestyle. In reality, they want a motorized extension of themselves. Let's look at what kind of buyers buy what kind of vehicle.

- **New.** The same group of financially well-heeled people always purchase a new car. New vehicle appearance is a major part of the purchase decision process in first-tier buyers, and is used as a success statement. Even though they could lose thousands of dollars at trade-in time, it all comes down to image and perceived value.

  General Motors was the perceived value leader in the 1950s and 60s. Today it is Lexus and Toyota. Even with the recent product recalls, Toyota has been able to retain and hold resale prices.

- **Value.** The second-tier of buyers are looking for value, and spend their money on solid, two- to three-year old, well-maintained vehicles. These vehicles have already depreciated almost one-third of their value, but are extremely clean and have very few miles on them. Make, color and appearance are still a major part of the purchase decision process.

- **Function.** Third-tier buyers purchase the five- and six-year old vehicles that have gone through at least two-thirds of their depreciation. These vehicles have some nicks and scratches, but have a good 30,000 to 60,000 usable miles left on them, with some mechanical repairs required. Vehicles in this range are still considered a reasonable transportation value for the buck. They are purchased much more for their functional value than their styling value.

A vehicle lifespan used to be about seven to twelve years before it reached the scrap yard. Today's vehicles are being better manufactured and are lasting at least three to five years longer.

• **Dust and Rust.** Usually the fourth-tier buyer is purchasing a totally whipped vehicle, not one previously driven by a retired schoolteacher. Used car dealers would normally call this vehicle a Transportation Special. It is also classified as a D&R (Dust and Rust), based on the dirt, rust, and body panel proliferation. The D&R vehicle cost is very low, but the repairs to keep the vehicle running are expensive. At this point in time, vehicle styling has been totally lost in the process of traveling from point A to point B. In most cases, people purchasing D&R vehicles are living just above the poverty line.

TRENDS

When trying to talk future design trends, it is best to look back to the past to understand how the whole trend in styling got started.

When it comes to style and trends, the automotive industry is very similar to the fashion industry. In clothing, designers provide fashion trends that look good on a wide variety of people, but that last for only a year or two. Some things, however, like blue jeans, will never go out of style—they are a true American classic. I would put the original Volkswagen Beetle in the same class as blue jeans.

Since automotive styling applies to a more durable product, it generally functions in the marketplace for a five- to ten-year timeframe. For example, the tailfin was first applied to the 1947 Cadillac, and culminated with the 1959 Cadillac. The Cadillac Motor Car Division maintained some sort of tailfin well into the mid 1960s.

WOODWARD DREAM CRUISE

Many vehicles that are considered classics today appear as examples of Detroit's past leadership in automotive design at the Woodward Dream Cruise. The Annual Woodward Dream Cruise is held every year in Michigan on the 3rd Saturday in August. The Woodward Dream Cruise runs from 9 a.m. to 9 p.m. along Woodward
Avenue through nine communities, from Ferndale in the south, to Pontiac at the north end. The event attracts more then 1 1/2 million people each year. To me, the Woodward Dream Cruise is a tribute to the American auto industries achievements of the 20th century.

However, anyone viewing the Woodward Dream Cruise will note there is an almost total lack of Ford Falcons, early Dodge Darts and Chevrolet Vegas, also cars of the 1950s, 60s and 70s. These vehicles did not capture the hearts and minds of the classic car collector. In the 2010 Woodward Dream Cruise, there was one Chevrolet Vega, with a big V-8 and the supercharger sticking up through the hood. This Vega was a squirrel car, not a classic.

At 73, I would probably be considered a dinosaur of the past who grew up in the age where everything connected to the auto industry had to get bigger and more powerful each year. And it would have continued if the 1973 oil embargo had not occurred.

Today I embrace fuel economy, but I also feel that vehicle size has to be safe, functional and capable of hauling a few people and a week's worth of groceries.

When it comes to classic Cars, my pride and joy is our 1976 Cadillac Eldorado convertible. I had worked for the Cadillac Motor Car Division in one of my early assignments. Part of my job was costing out the 500-cubic inch displacement (CID) engine. The engine was originally designed to be raised in size to 700 cubic inches. I've always been loyal and a dedicated fan of Cadillac and that is why I chose to purchase and rebuild one of the last Cadillac big convertibles. We enjoy taking our grandchildren on the Woodward Dream Cruise every year.

Del and Jan's 1976 Cadillac Eldorado

I use GM Design as a primary example because in my 32 years at GM, I was continually in the various studios. During my brief stint with Ford, I was also the liaison engineer for the Delta (Falcon) vehicle with Ford Design Studio. At Chrysler, where I spent eight years, I also made many trips to Chrysler's new Design Staff facilities attached to the sprawling Chrysler Technical Center in Auburn Hills, Michigan. On the CCV (Composite Concept Vehicle) project I would visit the studio to review the full-size clay model when it was under development. Bryan Nesbitt was the lead designer in the studio where the clay model for the lightweight plastic car for China was developed. Bryan was an up-and-coming designer at Chrysler when he was picked up by GM.

Vehicles with high horsepower engines and a sexy body surface end up 30 to 40 years later as classics. There are specific vehicles from Ford, GM, and Chrysler that have captured the hearts and souls of classic car collectors everywhere. Classic car collectors are passionate when they put down thousands of dollars to purchase a vehicle at Berrett-Jackson collector car auctions. It is the classic cars built by the Detroit's Big Three in the 1950s, 60s, and 70s that bring most of the excitement and money.

There is a certain charisma that makes people want a classic vehicle. Sometimes it's an expression of their youth, sometimes it's a status symbol. The trouble is, there are more people wanting certain specific vehicles of their youth than were manufactured. That is why the prices of some classic cars in pristine condition are becoming outrageous.

Automotive design is a matter of personal style and taste. The Detroit Big Three design studios turned a few of the dullest and ugliest vehicles in the 1970s, 80s, and 90s. Many feel some of the various design organizations wanted to retaliate against the U.S. government's Motor Vehicle Safety Standards (MVSS) with ugly bumper designs.

THE EVOLUTION OF AUTOMOBILE DESIGN

Engineers designed every aspect of vehicle function and appearance until the late 1920s. True design began in 1927 when Harley J. Earl styled the LaSalle as a less expensive alternative to the Cadillac. The 1927 LaSalle was the first fully-surfaced vehicle designed by a stylist.

General Motors was the first automotive company to lead the way and demonstrate an experimental test vehicle with advanced styling cues, starting in 1938 with Harley Earl's Buick Y-Job. After that, all of the Detroit Big Three began to build one-off experimental styling vehicles.

See a photo of Harley Earl in the Y-Job at www. gmphotostore.com/1938-Buick-Y-Job-and-Harley-Earl/productinfo/53217749/

It would not be until the late 1960s that stylists were called designers. In the 50s, the word "styling" started to sound synonymous with body surface entertainment. All of the Detroit Big Three changed the Styling Staff Divisional name to the Design Staff to be more in line with the function being preformed. Vehicle styling itself evolved by integrating the body surface with the vehicle's function.

Harley Earl

Harley Earl was a visionary, a leader, and truly a giant of the industry. Automotive styling all started with Harley J. Earl, and pivoted around him for about 30 years. In the beginning, most of the initial stylists were employees of Harley Earl's Art and Color staff, and trained by Harley personally. They later went on to the other automotive manufactures in the 1930s, like Auburn, Chrysler, Cord, Duesenberg, Ford, Hudson, Hupmobile, Nash, Packard, Pierce- Arrow, REO, and Studebaker. Harley trained many of both Ford and Chrysler's styling executives and vice presidents of design.

WHAT IT WAS LIKE WORKING IN A DESIGN STUDIO

In past years, the ambition for any red-blooded American as a transportation design student was to work for the Detroit Big Three. It was quite the achievement, as only five to eight designers were hired each year by each of the design staffs of the Detroit Big Three.

The best place to work in 1958 (GM's 50th birthday) was General Motors because GM used to have the largest design firm in the world under one roof, about 80-plus designers. The design firm was located at the GM

Technical Center in Warren, Michigan. Next was Ford Styling Center in Dearborn, Michigan; then Chrysler Styling Center, which at that time was in Highland Park, Michigan; and finally American Motors in Detroit.

By the time the Firebird III was completed in 1958, GM's Styling people were all sketching cars with a jet aircraft motif. People viewing a Firebird III today—over 50 years later—still find the vehicle awe-inspiring. No one in the entire auto industry has dared to go as far as GM reached then. The Firebird III did not have a steering wheel: it had a steering knob on the center console developed with the help of human factors engineers at GM Styling Staff. It was similar to the 2007 Mercedes Benz SCL 600 Concept vehicle shown to the public a full 49 years later. The standards set by Harley Earl and his team still outshine today's designers in some areas.

> When I joined GM's Styling Staff in 1960, we were given all new materials. More than I had ever seen. The new hire had many more art materials that even the wealthiest student could afford.

> For more information on the Firebird III, see http://en.wikipedia.org/wiki/General_Motors_Firebird.

DESIGNING VEHICLES USING THE COMPUTER

It was in 1984 that Steve Pasteiner became the first automotive designer I know of that experimented using a computer to design cars. When the project was shown to GM's Design VP, Irv Rybicki, he said, "Nice job, but someday we'll have holograms." The concept went completely over Irv's head because designers sketched vehicles with pencils. Steve Pasteiner also designed and built his own 2-seat sports car. Steve left GM Design Staff in 1989 to start his own company, AAPCars.com.

By the early 1990s, a GM automotive designer by the name of Charles H. Graef III started to illustrate sketches on the computer. Charlie used Silicon Graphics hardware. Using the computer, automotive designs could be altered and up-dated quickly. Charlie Graef III truly began the transition of designing cars by sketching with pencils to designing vehicles with mouse clicks.

By the late 1990s, automobile design centers around the world were completely shifting to the computer. They also began using digitized data to sculpt clay models. Using the computer to provide the digitized data, clay models could be prepared faster for viewing. Designers still feel clay sculptures are required to tweak, correct, or read a full-size visual surface.

DESIGN STAFF VIEWING AREA

Most designers prefer to view the full-size vehicles or clay models in natural sunlight to make an assessment on how the vehicle will appear to the customer. All of the Detroit Big Three have walled-in, brick-paved, outdoor viewing areas with accenting trees. They are large enough for designers to get some distance, which is necessary for making a proper visual assessment. The standard saying was "take the clay outside." Viewing the model inside the confines of the studio was like "trying to judge a horse in the kitchen."

THE NATURAL FLOW OF DESIGN TALENT

There is a normal flow of automotive designers through the various Detroit Big Three Design Centers. When new designers enter the auto industry, they all want to design sports cars like Corvettes, T-Birds, and Vipers. The sad truth is that there is very little need to have designers designing sports cars because they are low volume vehicles with the body styling designed to last ten years. For example, the Corvette was introduced in 1953: in 2011, by my count, the Corvette has had only five major chassis designs and nine major body surfaces. Nevertheless, many minor design tweaks are needed to give yearly identity.

For the most part, designers work on the major body surfaces every four to six years, with minor styling changes each year. Sometimes designers will spend years working on a certain assignment, such as aluminum wheels or hubcap design. The wheel surface is 15 to 18 inches in diameter, allowing for the different arrangement and number of spokes. When you think of the challenge of arranging spokes and holes to make each new wheel design more exciting than last year's model, you've got quite a challenge. Some talented designers felt stifled having to work on wheels, hood ornamentation, and other vehicle appliques for weeks and months on end. Many left just to seek change and a greater opportunity elsewhere. For example, Bryan Nesbitt, who was an excellent designer at Chrysler, was picked up by GM Design Staff. Today Bryan Nesbitt is a GM Design Staff Vice President.

CREATING MARKET NICHES

In the first 100 years of the automotive industry, Ford was the hands-down leader in starting and establishing many new market niches. Ford led in 1908 with the Model T for the common man; in 1927 with the Model A; then in 1932 with the Model B, which included a low-cost optional V-8 engine on entry-level vehicles. The 1958 Ford Thunderbird then went on to lead the personal luxury car market niche. GM followed in 1963 with the Buick Riviera, in 1966 with the Oldsmobile Tornado, and in 1967 with the Cadillac Eldorado. With the success of the personal luxury market, mid-luxury vehicles came out: the Pontiac Grand Prix in 1969 and the Chevrolet Monte Carlo in 1970.

The 1965 Ford Mustang created the personal 2 + 2 Pony Car niche. Two years later, GM introduced their Mustang look-alikes, the 1967 Chevrolet Camaro and the Pontiac Firebird. It took the Chrysler Corporation until 1970 to respond with their two Pony Cars: the Plymouth Barracuda (later to be called just Cuda) and the Dodge Challenger. Also that year, AMC Corporation produced their version, called the Javelin. In 2005, the lone survivor in the original Pony Car niche was the Ford Mustang, later re-joined by GM's Chevrolet Camaro in 2009 and the Dodge Challenger in 2010.

Ford has also led in the econovan and pick-up truck market niche.

The Chrysler minivan was the brainchild of former Ford executive Hal Sperlich. Unable to sell the minivan concept to Henry Ford II, he brought the idea with him when he joined the Chrysler Corporation as it was unraveling in late 1970s.

It is rumored that Hal was also instrumental in bringing Lee Iacocca to the Chrysler Corporation in 1978. Both Lee Iacocca and the minivan saved the Chrysler Corporation in the 1980s.

In the 21st century, the design rage has been crossovers. To me, a crossover has the combined features of a van, an SUV and a station wagon, all wrapped into one and downsized. Other models have been designed to appeal to the 65 and older crowd. Bryan Nesbitt designed a geriatric vehicle for Chrysler that was labeled by the Human Factors group as the "tall car" because the vehicle's entrance was higher than normal for ease of entrance and egress.

DaimlerChrysler brought their "older crowd" vehicle out as the PT Cruiser. Interestingly, the PT Cruiser appealed to the younger crowd as a retro cult vehicle rather than a geriatric vehicle.

GM dropped their original design for a tall car, but later designed the Chevrolet HHR as a retro cult vehicle with some of the features that the older crowd liked. Ironically it was Bryan Nesbitt that was the prime design person on both the HHR and the PT Cruiser.

GM TRIES TO CREATE A MARKET NICHE

General Motors tried to create an image vehicle for Pontiac after the demise of the Pontiac Fiero. A car division like Chevrolet has the Corvette as the image vehicle to bring people into the showroom. where they may purchase a more functional family vehicle.

In 1990, I was put in charge of the Pontiac Stinger Program. This was a fun vehicle that looked like a cross between a Corvette and a Jeep. To me, the vehicle was beautiful—but every parent thinks their children are beautiful. I wanted to change the identification name from Stinger to something more positive. I did not want to have someone say, "I bought a Pontiac Stinger, and I got Stung."

The project was killed due to lack of corporate funds, but in reality I felt there were no longer risk-takers in GM's upper management. At that point, we were asked to see if we could develop an image vehicle for Pontiac by putting some cladding on a GEO Tracker. We put a GEO Tracker on the surface plate and tried to apply clay. It was a dumb project so we dubbed the vehicle BOHICA. We said we named the vehicle after the great Chief BOHICA of the Ottawa tribe, the same tribe that Chief Pontiac came from. In reality BOHICA means, "Bend Over, Here It Comes Again." The BOHICA project died a slow natural death because of little interest and no key support.

For more about the Pontiac Stinger, see http://auto.howstuffworks.com/1989-pontiac-stinger-concept-car.htm.

BULDING A BETTER CAR

Ford and General Motors design studios need to put life and style back into their vehicle line-up. In the last few years Ford has improved the most. GM has updated the Cadillac and Buick lines to improve customer interest. Cadillac has their own identity with unique, edgy styling. Chrysler had the styling edge in the late 1980s and 1990s under VP of Design Tom Gale, who is now long gone—and so has the luster of Chrysler's design.

For Ford and GM to regain a foothold and take over the vehicle design leadership, bold design surfaces will have to be created by the people already in place. The suggested cooperation of Ford and General Motors' Engineering and Manufacturing operations would include the design studios in the merger process. World design (styling) leadership needs to return to the last, two, true American automobile manufacturers.

The combined design, engineering and manufacturing operations need to design vehicles that are more sophisticated and dynamic in appearance than any other vehicle on the road today, vehicle shapes that say, "I MUST HAVE IT." Cars should look to be full of spirit and fun to drive, like the 1965 Ford Mustang was in its time. The new design team will have to take an offensive position, where the design of the vehicles looks like they are in motion when they are at rest. In 2011, Korean manufactures Kia and Hyundai have made the best attempt of capturing the look of a vehicle in motion while sitting still.

It is design excitement and passion that needs to be rekindled by the new Ford and GM design team. It goes without saying that the new Ford and General Motors Design team must be led by a design leader that has a total passion for designing exciting vehicles.

What follows are some of my own design suggestions:

There is a need to design body surfaces that flow and create motion while standing still. Vehicle shape must inspire motion: a car is a transportation vehicle for moving people and goods. Remember, **"Form Must Follow Function,"** a statement always made when new employees joined GM Styling's Research Studio.

Harley Earl's directions to follow **aircraft design** is still a pretty good direction when it comes to free flowing designs. The 2009 Nissan Maxima design team claim they drew inspiration from the SR-71 CIA reconnaissance spy plane.

Aerodynamics will play a principle part of all future automotive designs because fuel efficiency is now a major factor when purchasing a vehicle, due to high fuel prices. In the near future, the vehicle aerodynamic Coefficient of Drag, or Cd number, will be posted on the window sticker along with city and highway mileage numbers.

CHROME IS STILL IDENTIFIED WITH AUTOMOBILE DESIGN

The Chrome 50s transitioned into the flowing organic surfaces (Ford Taurus) of the 1980s. And there is still a tendency to plaster chrome on vehicles: look at the 2009 Cadillac with the flat chrome plate above the rear license plate as a throwback to more glorious times. In 2011, most vehicles have adapted a large, chrome cross-piece above the rear license plate. In the 50s, Buick had portholes on the front fenders—today everyone has vents on the front fender as a styling trend that I acknowledge as just surface entertainment.

SEAMLESSLY FLOWING INTO ORGANIC SHAPES

Mr. Hulki Aldikacti was an executive at Pontiac who initiated the soft fascia concept on an experimental 1971 Pontiac Firebird to keep the car in production. Paul Haines of the Inland Division of GM and I were some of the leaders on the manufacturing team that helped make that transition happen. The first two applications of the soft fascia were with the 1973 Corvette front bumper fascia and the 1973 Pontiac Grand Am front bumper. I was persuasive enough to talk the Executive Director of Manufacturing Staff to pay for the 1973 Corvette front bumper tooling out of his budget to push the soft fascia project along. Today almost every car built on this planet has a soft fascia bumper system. The soft fascia bumper business now amounts to over $12 billion annually. Why? Because the body of a car is like a loaf of bread, and by changing the ends (new fascia front and rear) every year, a whole new appearance is achieved for a fraction of the old cost. Also, the previous design consisted of many parts that were consolidated into one very cost effective part. It always comes down to the bottom line. The soft fascia enabled automobile manufactures to meet Motor Vehicle Safety Standards (MVSS) and a cost savings at the same time.

When it comes to automotive design trends, the Detroit Big Three design centers have all been through a few. The chrome-cladding phase of the 40s and 50s; the tail fin and continental tire kit phase of the 50s and 60s; the jelly bean phase of the 70s and 80s, into the flowing organic surfaces (Ford Taurus) of the 1980s; the sharp edge design and box-like phase of the late 1990s and so far into the 2000s. The next trend is still on the computer screen, but will be out soon.

When it comes to speeds above 50 mph, aerodynamic principles are already in play. Designers of today understand aerodynamic principles because they work directly in the wind tunnel, changing body surfaces. Clay models can be tweaked in the throat of the wind tunnel in a matter of minutes.

With the push for active aerodynamics on all vehicles, the use of the flexible/collapsible urethane side enclosure concept will come into play.

Body panels can be overlapping—the front fender will overlap the door to improve the aerodynamics of the door gap. The underbody of the vehicle will be designed mostly smooth, with the vehicle body lowering to less than three to four inches off the road, even at surface speeds greater than 50 mph. Some luxury brand vehicles can do that today.

In 2008, BMW designed a test vehicle with **fabric body panels**. A concept of this nature would add to changing vehicle shape to improve aerodynamics while the vehicle is moving. As the automobile industry approaches a green vehicle, a recycled fabric mesh might be the answer. Body tooling costs could be greatly reduced; the body skin could be fabric similar to a convertible top but much thinner and softer. (For more about the BMW GINA, see http://en.wikipedia.org/wiki/BMW_GINA.)

Some engineers think BMW's stretchable fabric surfaces will lead to slightly heavier vehicle structures, especially when considering crash requirements and the mechanism required to move the surfaces. Only time will tell.

Note: It's not by coincidence that bird feathers are layered in an overlapping quilted pattern. The same principles apply. Again, it's Mother Nature at her engineering best.

Photovoltaic solar collectors could be shaped like a snakeskin platelets or sharkskin dentricals to give a better aerodynamic flow. Body surfaces that are not totally smooth will come into play when body surface and attached airflow are better understood. The sharkskin surface has dentricals, considered a directional friction material, to cause turbulence in the water directly contacting the sharkskin. Attached flow give higher surface drag over every square inch of body surface where the dentricals reduce surface drag, allowing the shark to swim faster with less effort.

Vortex generators (the little trapezoid blades placed on a Boeing 707 wing) strategically placed on the vehicle surface can direct the airflow. The vortex generators help at varying wind direction yaw angles because cars are always driving in crosswinds. Some corporations designed heavy-duty aero trucks with vortex generators in the 1980s, but none made production.

Also, as manufactures push for greater fuel economy, many small design changes will occur. In the next five years vehicles will develop **spats**, both in front and behind each road wheel, to improve aerodynamic efficiency. Also, vehicles will have little lips or ridges attached to the body to reduce

I worked on a convertible top Patent Number 5941595, METHOD AND APPARATUS FOR REDUCING LIFT AND DRAG of a soft-top passenger vehicle. The last bow on the convertible top is made to have a higher ridge cap that protrudes into the air stream by 3/8 inch to improve convertible aerodynamics by reducing attached flow when the top is up.

Note: Useful trivia information when driving at 90 MPH. Today, a vehicle traveling 90 mph uses over 80% of its fuel to move the air up, around and over the vehicle; less than 20% of the fuel consumed is used to move the vehicle.

attached airflow. The same principle applies to convertible tops.

The Chrysler Crossfire had an **active rear spoiler** that tilts up at speeds greater than 35 mph. Active aero is a far more efficient approach to provide more aerodynamically advantageous shapes than using a fixed reinforced plastic surface. Active aero can deform under aerodynamic loading and use the fiber orientation to allow tailoring of the deformed shape. Formula 1 race cars are banned from using active aero, but some are using technology to cheat the rule. I also believe some stealth aircraft also use the active aero technique.

In the future, the **exterior body surface** could be covered with photovoltaic solar collectors to add electrical capacity to the on-board battery/generation system. Solar collectors running in full sunlight could charge the vehicle even while the vehicle is running, adding to the overall vehicle range and efficiency. New nano-technologies creating photovoltaic in a printable or paintable material would probably be the way to efficiently apply solar technology to intricate surfaces. Glass coatings are also being developed, so solar collecting surfaces can be maximized.

Paint colors themselves will vary by the sunlight intensity and angle. The new pearlized and metallic exterior colors are outstanding and very popular. Some corporations already have some blues that turn reddish purple at dusk.

In the near future, all **windows** on the vehicle could take on the vehicle body color. The window surface will appear to blend into the body without a seam in some areas and have a trip-lip in non-vision areas to reduce attached airflow. The windshield glass will wrap around into the door covering the "A" pillar. Oldsmobile built the Tornado with rear window glass the same way, without the "C" pillar (rear pillar). The "A" pillar (front pillar) will be behind the glass. GM's Opel division has already built an experiential vehicle using this principle. (The "B" pillar is between the front and rear doors.)

Interiors. Vehicle interiors vary in appearance. Those with metal plates with lighting holes for the clutch, brake, and accelerator pedal are definitely male-oriented. Women would be afraid to get a heel caught in one of those little holes. Women also need an accessible hook on the underside of the instrument panel on the passenger side to be able to conveniently hook their purse. This way the purse will be fully accessible and visible in a convenient location.

Bill Mitchell, the second vice president of GM's Design Staff, caught a Macko Shark on a vacation. That's how it became the vision for the experimental Corvette fish series of vehicles. The 1961 experimental Corvette Macko Shark One was designed by Larry Shinoda, along with the 1963 Corvette production Stingray. Sticking to the exotic fish motif, the production 1968 Corvette (Corvette code: C-3) again took its styling cues from the Bill Mitchell's Macko Shark II. What a beauty.

The goal of the interior environment is to offer a safe, functional appearance. The addition of side impact airbags add a great deal in selling safety to the customer. Safety is also where the driver can reach and identify all of the buttons and knobs easily while driving. The interior of the vehicle with its safety seatbelt and airbag system will provide that cocoon of protection every driver needs. Interiors will continue to become softer, easier to clean, and less sun reflection in the future. The interior will flow seamlessly from one area and function to the other.

THE BOX

Many the aerodynamics principles must be adhered to even when designing a box. Note the box vehicles all have nice, nine-inch, diameter round leading edges for aerodynamics reasons. The box shape is designed like an aerody-namic brick.

Ford's FLEX copied Toyota's and Honda's youth economy box vehicles. The box shape is a small trend, and it will probably not take over. However, it appears functional for hauling stuff and might someday even be considered a cult vehicle, like the VW Van of the 50s and 60s.

Heads-up **displays** with the speedometer and other vehicle warning information projected on the windshield surface (just like military jet aircraft) could become the norm in the future. With the advent of so much computer technology becoming integrated into the vehicle, such as the navigation system, there is a need to make the technology and the system more user-friendly. The computer geniuses that design these systems need to consider the skills of the users, especially the senior citizens who can afford them, but find understanding and using them a challenge. Vehicles still have to be designed for 73-year-old curmudgeons like me.

We have received from the **Lookoutamerica.org** website many personal pet peeves about the interiors of modern mainstream automobiles. Consumers think that interior designers could do much more to make even a mid-level interior look and feel "rich." Complaints focus around surface material that looks and feels cheap. And there's the squeak-rattle issue that just isn't up to well-made car standards.

Interior material developers who can successfully imitate the look, feel, and craftsmanship of the Bentley, in a sleek, not over-stuffed look, will really get a marketing advantage. When designers figure out how to push the plush-looking materials into the less expensive cars, they'll provide the greatest marketing advantage. Chevrolet has pushed interior upgrading and improved the 2010 Malibu.

Safety. Each year, on average, over 42,000 people lose their lives on U.S. highways, more than ten times the death rate from military action

In 1979, I was assigned Staff Engineer in charge of GMC Truck and Coach Body Engineering for the Low Cab Forward, Medium Duty and Astro Truck Body. We embarked on developing an aerodynamic heavy duty cab-over engine truck called the Aero Astro that improved fuel economy by over 25%. Photo: Prototype vehicle, Aero Astro Truck Cab.

on an annual basis.[1] Yet, today's race car drivers can survive impacts of

over 100 mph range with ease. Only when the public demands and is willing to pay the price for occupant safety, will major changes occur. When the primary focus when purchasing a new vehicle starts to shift and center around occupant safety, greater passenger survivability will be developed in crashes in the 50- to 65-mph range. I feel that within the next five to ten years, safety features centering on occupant safety in crashes up to 65 mph will become the primary focus when purchasing a new vehicle.

THE ESSENCE OF DESIGN

> *The future is not some place we are going, but one we are creating. The paths are not to be found, but made. And the activity of making them changes both the maker and their destination. —John Schaar*

Style and design are paramount to the marketing and selling of vehicles. Companies that provide stylish vehicles built with quality and at an affordable price will garnish a lion's share of the market place and become the value leader.

It's really that simple.

---

1 In 2010, the number of automotive-related deaths dropped over previous years. I believe this is due to improvement in side airbag application to more vehicles.

Over the years I have always run a Skunk Works operation as part of the regular departmental operation. A Skunk Works is a half-sanctionedand half-illicit operation. Any project was fair game, as long as it was not illegal, immoral or fattening. Project monies were set aside to be used

with no questions asked. Everything was run based on trust. The friendly fender (bases of the Saturn car), the fiberglass leaf springs used on 50% of all GM cars, the Honeycomb E/A system used on light GM cars, Fiberglass Heavy Duty Truck cabs, along with the fiberglass bumper beam are just few of the Skunk Works projects.

Peppy Le Pew was our mascot and was featured on lapel pin to be worn under the shirt collar or suit coat collar. I used to go to a Skunk Camp hosted by the Tom Peters Group and meet people from other industries running Skunk Works operations.

My 1962 red Aurora project.

In 1963, modifications included a color change to Fire Mist Silver.

MY PERSONAL 1961 AURORA CORVETTE

In 1961, as a young designer, I took the summer off to build my own personal sports car after looking at all of the experimental cars at GM Styling Staff. As a mechanical engineering and automotive design student at Michigan State University, I had previously designed a 1/10 scale clay model of my ideal sports car.

I designed the car as a convertible with a removable fast-back hardtop. I called it the "Aurora," which was my statement for the beginning of a new era—and it was, for me. Thirty-four years later, the Oldsmobile Division used the Aurora name for their replacement vehicle for the Toronado.

Not only did building the Aurora give me a sense of pride and enjoyment, I gained the hands-on experience of building it myself, and it greatly helped me in my understanding of vehicles.

Then, in 1964 ... a blue convertible.

PART THREE: TECHNOLOGY AND TRANSPORTATION

INNOVATIONS OF THE PAST AND PRESENT IN THE AUTO INDUSTRY

THE OIL/FUEL DILEMMA

TRANSPORTATION AND THE FUTURE

NEW ALTERNATIVE ENERGY

INNOVATIONS OF THE PAST AND PRESENT IN THE AUTO INDUSTRY

It is not good enough for things to be planned—they still have to be done; for the intention to become a reality, energy has to be launched into operation. —Pir Vilayat Khan

BUILDING A BETTER CAR

Some people are under the impression planet Earth is in a crisis created and perpetuated by humans; others claim that global warming is just a natural part of the Earth/sun cycle of heat exchange. Either way, the fact is that climate change is occurring and the man-made concentration of greenhouse gases called CO_2 and CH_4 only add to the problem.

The EPA has required a new car window sticker that will go into effect for the 2013 model year. Fuel economy and air pollution for 15,000 miles will be predominately displayed in an effort to keep the consumer more informed on the vehicles environmental impact.

Every person on Earth should contribute to reduce greenhouse warming. A focal part of this chapter will be to point out the ways Ford and GM can build personal transportation that will contribute to a total reduction of CO_2 emissions. To win back old customers and make new ones, Ford and General Motors need to establish quality vehicle technologies that uniformly reduce fuel consumption and the output of CO_2 emissions as their contribution to preserve the planet. The goal is to become a green company and totally embrace the environment.

To Put the Future of Transportation into Perpective, a Review of the Past Is Necessary

The history of personal transportation has been totally remarkable considering all of the changes that have taken place in such a short period of time. When the Declaration of Independence was signed in 1776, man's personal transportation was limited to horses or mules, horse drawn carriages, and ships with sails. Steam-powered trains and boats weren't invented yet.

Henry Ford founded the Ford Motor Car Company in 1903. Henry Ford's goal was to design automobiles for the masses, and with that vision he initially controlled over 50% of the market. Henry Ford was definitely an anomaly among early automotive creators, and he proved to be quite a visionary.

The General Motors Company was formed by Billy Durant when he consolidated the existing automobile companies of Buick and Oldsmobile in 1908,. The Dodge Brothers formed Dodge Motors in 1915 after a split and lawsuit with the Ford Motor Car Company. Walter P. Chrysler formed the Chrysler Corporation in 1924. Dodge Motors was purchased in 1927 by Walter P. Chrysler to add to the nucleus of the Chrysler Corporation. These three companies all struggled, merged, and added additional automotive manufacturing facilities to become what was known by the 1950s as the Big Three: Ford, General Motors, and Chrysler.

The U.S. auto industry started building war equipment and munitions for the United States government in the early 1940s as a total support effort for World War II. Many in the industry considered the rapid conversion of over 1,000 manufacturing operations into the "Arsenal of Democracy" a great act of patriotism. Truly, it is one of the 20th century's most outstanding industrial accomplishments.

World War II brought the beginning of the end of The Great Depression. The efforts of the American auto industry and their ability to mass-produce enough weapons to defeat both Germany and Japan helped contribute to the end of the war and of the depression. Sixty years later, both Germany and Japan are allies of the United States and both are hurting the U.S. auto industry economically.

AUTOMOTIVE INNOVATION IN THE 20TH CENTURY

Internal Combustion Engine Vehicles. The internal combustion engine (ICE) has been the mainstay power plant for the automobile industry for the last 100 years.

In the 1930s, the maximum number of cylinders increased to 16 as the luxury car manufacturers tried to out do each other and differentiate themselves from the also ran with V-12 and V-16 engine offerings. The V-8 was introduced into the high-volume, low-end market by Henry Ford in his new Model-B in 1932. By the 1950s, almost every automaker offered V-8s across their product line-up. Chevrolet introduced their small block V-8 with the design team lead by Ed Cole in 1955, and it was an instant success. More smaller block Chevrolet V-8 engines have been built than any other V-8 engine in the world. Over 50 years later, the same basic Chevrolet engine is still being built today.

However, with the OPEC oil embargoes in 1973 and 1979, the Big Three started to design vehicles with smaller engines. By the 1980s, auto manufactures had switched out most of their V-8 to V-6 engines in an effort to produce lighter weight and higher mileage vehicles.

Gas Turbine Engines. The closest any auto manufacture ever came to the production of a gas turbine vehicle was in 1965. The Chrysler Corporation built over 50 vehicles to be put into the driving public's hands for evaluation. All Chrysler gas turbine vehicles were easily identifiable not only by their unique body style, but also by their copper-colored paint. Most people were favorably impressed by the vehicles gas turbine performance and did not consider the vacuum cleaner hum objectionable.

Ford Motor Car Company's gas turbine research efforts were primarily handled by their Research and Scientific Laboratory Staff, where I worked in 1967 and 1968.

Based on high manufacturing costs and poor fuel efficiency, the production of a gas turbine powered vehicle was always questionable. Most work on gas turbine engines for automotive applications was halted at the start of the first OPEC oil embargo in 1973.

How Regenerative Braking Works

For a long time engineers have been troubled by vehicle braking as wasted energy. Accelerating from a stop position to highway speed is the highest energy demand load a vehicle is faced with. Regenerative breaking is defined as breaking energy that is captured and turned back into useful power to be later used to assist in the acceleration of the vehicle.

There is more than one way to capture braking energy. The two most popular methods are electric generators and hydraulic accumulators. Flywheels and rubber bands can be coupled as a secondary power to the internal combustion engine. The best part is that the latest and greatest braking technology is yet to come from our grandchildren, those guys running around the house in diapers.

EPA PUTS GOALS INTO EFFECT BY 1975

The United States Environmental Protection Agency (EPA) was created in July, 1970, under the Nixon Administration.

In 1973, an "oil embargo" was created by the Organization of Petroleum Exporting Countries (OPEC) because they wanted to bring up the selling price of oil to compensate for the constant devaluation of the U.S. dollar. In response, two years later the EPA mandated fuel economy standards onto the American car-buying public and all automotive manufactures selling vehicles in the U.S. to reduce fuel consumption.

Manufactures were given a ten-year time span to make incremental improvements and eventually reach the mandated goal of 27.5 miles per gallon (mpg), the Corporate Average Fuel Economy (CAFE) Standard.

At the time of the Oil Embargo, General Motors manufactured a 1973 Buick Roadmaster that weighed in at over two tons and got less than 13 mpg. There was a lot of belly-aching by all of the Big Three about the monies it was going to cost the corporations to meet the newly imposed standards by 1985.

In 2009, the same 1985 EPA CAFE Standards were still in effect—it's 24 years later and there's no change. No one in government felt additional CAFE Standards were needed! Maybe the U.S. Congress was in bed with Big Oil? Look at the Congressional hearings held in Washington in May of 2011, questioning the billions of dollars in tax breaks given over the years to Big Oil when they are so profitable. Maybe it's all about lobbyist and campaign donations? You think! Or maybe, the U.S. auto industry kept saying, *It costs too much*, like the Bryon of 1980.

THE LEAN MACHINES

By the 1990s, there were a variety of three- and four-wheel vehicles that were small and lean like motorcycles—pointing out the fuel savings capabilities while also demonstrating the value of reduced cabin space if there was a need for only one rider.

Electric Vehicles

The Lunar Rover. In early 1970s, General Motors built the first vehicle to travel on the surface of the moon. The vehicle was called the Lunar Rover. The Lunar Rover was powered by electric motors, one in each wheel assembly. The tires and wheels were an integral metal spring assembly of wire mesh and titanium chevrons for traction in the moonscape's soft soil.

Apollo flights 15, 16, and 17 all used Lunar Rover vehicles. Of the total of seven functional Lunar Rovers that were built for NASA, three still sit on the moon's surface today. With no atmosphere on the moon, the Lunar Rovers and their tire tracks will be there for thousands of years to come. A total of eight Lunar Rovers, including an initial test-bed vehicle, were built by GM's Delco Electronics.

It is hard to believe that all those years ago GM was able to design an electric vehicle that operated flawlessly on the lunar surface of the moon. Today, after a false start in 1996 with the EV1, GM has finally come up with a salable electric vehicle called the Chevrolet Volt—and the good news is that it runs on Earth's surface. It only took 40 years. Go figure!

GM Sunraycer. The GM Sunraycer was especially built to compete in the 1987 special solar vehicle race called the Great Solar Race. The race covered a total distance of 3,000 miles across the Austrian Outback. The GM Sunraycer was designed in a flat, pumpkin seed shape with voltaic solar cells on the top surface. GM Sunraycer crossed the finish line in first place a full two and a half days ahead of the second place competitor.

EV-1. GM introduced the EV-1 in 1996 to the California and Arizona automobile markets as a totally electric vehicle. The car was built and leased by GM, and its production plant in Lansing, Michigan was building four vehicles per day. When the EV-1 was introduced, and other automakers also introduced electric vehicles into the California market, the California Air Recourse Board (CARB) introduced new electric vehicle legislation. CARB made it mandatory that all manufactures selling vehicles in California had to have 2% of their sales zero emmision vehicles. The electric vehicle manufactures all folded their tent and quit selling electric vehicles. GM even crushed the entire fleet of EV-1's to destroy the possibility of ever returning to the California market. This measure prompted the movie, "Who Killed the Electric Car?"

It's a shame that General Motors and Ford blew a golden opportunity with electric vehicles and hybrids, turning the innovation into a media disaster. Rather than dealing with CARB on the magnitude and reality of the situation, they just quit. They ended up looking incapable of handling innovation that would improve the planet, and totally self serving.

While Toyota, Ford, and Honda closed their electric vehicle sales efforts because no one wanted to stand alone, Honda and Toyota continued their gasoline and electric hybrid vehicle programs and were the first to offer successful hybrid products to the automotive buying public. The Toyota Prius hybrid leads that market segment today.

GM's Hybrid Van Program. In the early 1990 time frame, GM's Research and Advanced Engineering people were building up three prototypes of an All Purpose Van (APV) hybrid vehicle. The goal was to utilize electrical components from GM's Electric Vehicle EV- 1, then still under development. When the three prototypes were built, by hand waving, the vice president of CPC Engineering requested that a set of backwards-engineering drawing be made: that way, if Detroit Edison, Consumers Power, or New York's Con Edison wanted a fleet of 400, GM's manufacturing people would have something to go on. I was given that assignment with the Pontiac Stinger personnel when the Pontiac Stinger vehicle was canceled. Ken Lane, one of our top designers helped to complete the task in record time as we built a parallel vehicle to verify assembly methods. All drawings for the hybrid APV Van were completed and placed on file, never to be heard from again because of the impending CARB legislation.

GEM Neighborhood Electric Vehicle. In 1998, when CARB legislated 2% of all vehicles sold in California had to meet the zero-emission goal, the entire auto industry panicked. Luckily for DaimlerChrysler AG (DCX), they'd purchased Global Electric Motors (GEM) in the late 1990s as a standby for just such an occasion. GEM had been looking for a White Knight, and the timing was perfect for both companies. When DCX acquired GEM they had an electric vehicle program in house instantly.

Over the years, DCX made minor improvements to the GEM vehicles, which look like over sized golf cart with doors that keep out the elements. GEM vehicles now have a wider array of customers because of their flexibility of configuration.

ECoV Electric. The EcoV Electric Vehicle is a unique and highly practical vehicle developed by Richard W. Marks of Grosse Pointe, Michigan. Richard worked on GM's EV-1 engineering team in the 1990s, and when the EV-1 was canceled, felt there was still a need for an electric delivery vehicle. Richard's EcoV is a lightweight, low-cost, electric vehicle designed for city and neighborhood driving situations. Seating four full-size adults, it is capable of carrying 1,000 pounds and can convert in seconds to a utility vehicle by folding the rear seat down into a storage platform. The EcoV is ideal for small businesses with lots of short-range deliveries. With a top speed of 25 mph by NSTA law, and a range is 40 miles, the EcoV can be re-charged off of 110 voltage. The EcoV is well thought-out, and has room to add a hybrid engine, if requested. Website: www.EcoV-Electric.com.

The Tesla Roadster. The Tesla Motors Team defied the auto industry by going where no one in the entire world's automotive industry has dared to tread—into the high performance and high-end of the electric vehicle market, that is. They broke through the mindset of current auto industry leaders who assumed that electric vehicles are for underachieving, save-the-world people. Tesla proved that even the rich want to be green.

Electric NASCAR. Imagine a time when NASCAR drivers get out of their hydrocarbon-consuming race cars and switch to electric vehicles just because they perform better and are faster. Then the race limitations will switch from engine displacement and fuel tank size to the electric motor and battery size. It will be like full-sized versions of the 1/24-scale model electric slot cars automotive engineers of the 1960s raced on weekends for fun and jollies. If Thomas E. Edison were alive today, he would be ecstatic about electric race cars.

Honda Insight Hybrid. In the Honda Insight Hybrid, the braking generator captures and stores electrical energy in special nickel metal hydride batteries with about 25-30% efficiency. When the accelerator pedal is depressed, the electric motor will drive the car at low speeds before the gasoline engine kicks in.

Toyota Prius Hybrid. One of the leading candidates for perceived fuel economy is the Toyota Prius. The Prius is a gasoline/electric hybrid that uses an electric generator/motor as a generator to absorb breaking loads. Toyota also covers the mid-sized market with its Camry hybrid, using Prius components.

Plug-In/CNG Hybrid. The natural gas hybrid vehicle is not only a very low emissions vehicle, but also a convenient vehicle as far as energy availability. For example, the plug-in electric battery charging connection for the primary system is located in the owner's garage. The electrical grid for charging the batteries is radio frequency activated to connect in off-load conditions. And the natural gas compressor provides CH4 fuel under pressure to fill the vehicles storage tanks for the secondary power source. The internal combustion engine finds its fuel also located in the garage. The natural gas internal combustion engine extends the vehicle range.

The battery charging system may use either 110 or 220 voltages from the house electrical system. This would make charging the hybrid battery system a simple matter of plugging in during non-peak hours. The natural gas can be compressed as CNG and stored in high pressure cylinders placed in the vehicle. Recent discoveries on U.S. soil of natural gas have shown an abundant supply, enough to last at least the entire 21st century.

At the present time there are a very limited number of vehicles that have been converted for CNG operation, with Honda Motors the leading pioneer. To add to the problem, there are very few natural gas refueling stations around the country. Even so, a CNG vehicle could be filled in the homeowner's garage on a "as need" basis. This would be ideal for over 90% of the vehicle's "useful driving cycle." At the present time, the comparable cost of CNG fuel is around $2.79—compared to a gallon of unleaded gasoline at $4.50 per gallon for the same mileage driven. Also, keep in mind that using CNG will require about four times the fuel tank volume to match the driving range of a similar gasoline-fueled vehicle: the fuel density ratio is 4 to 1.

Chevrolet Volt (PHEV). It was at the 2007 North American International Auto Show (NAIAS) that General Motors took a bold step by presenting the Chevrolet Volt, an electric/hybrid concept vehicle. It was a show-stopper based on both its good looks and its electrical technology.

The Volt was designed as a plug-in hybrid-electric vehicle (PHEV). It's considered a compact car, part of the E - Flex platform, and about the size of a Chevrolet Cobalt. The Volt can be 100% driven by a 149 HP gasoline engine when batteries are low. Electrical energy is supplied by a lithium ion battery pack.

One of the best things about the Volt it is an electric vehicle that won't leave you stranded when there is no more battery power. To the many engineers and GM team members that worked hard to make the vision of the Chevrolet Volt a production reality, *Job well done*.

The Hydraulic Hybrid. A 100% hydraulic vehicle system offers a whole new opportunity on total vehicle configuration. Every major vehicle function is handled hydraulically, from driving power to steering and braking. Power input can come from many sources—gasoline, diesel, and electric motors powered by batteries or by fuel cell.

The entire vehicle is run by a power plant driving a hydraulic pump that provides fluid power to a pump located at each wheel. The conventional driveline has been eliminated and replaced with a main driving pump connected to wheel driving pumps through hydraulic lines. With each wheel being driven independently, traction control, ABS braking, and forward and reverse can be accomplished with ease.

In the next chapter, I'll demonstrate how hybrid-type vehicles and fuel sources that could have a direct and positive effect on reducing greenhouse gases by over 50%.

THE ENERGY/FUEL DILEMMA

The Middle East oil situation for the last 38 years was captured so elegantly by renowned political cartoonist Jeff Stahler of the **Columbus Dispatch** in April 2011.

Prior to 1973, the price of a barrel of oil was pegged to the price of a bushel of wheat. Ever since the oil embargo imposed by traders and the Organization of Petroleum Exporting Countries (OPEC), speculation on a barrel of oil has caused the price to fluctuate all over the place, from a low of $2.75/bl in 1973, to over $10/bl at the start of 1974, to touching a high of $147/bl in 2008. Now in May of 2011, oil is $109/bl.

Today, the United States is importing about 60% of the oil it is consuming. All of this oil consumption is not free. The reality is that American citizens are transferring billions of dollars out of the U.S. economy to support this gluttony for large, inefficient vehicles. Only when the price of gasoline nears $4 per gallon do U.S. consumers start thinking fuel economy. Then, when the gasoline prices ease, consumer priorities swing back to larger vehicles again.

The American auto industry needs to set some dramatic, clear-cut goals to improve vehicle fuel economy and reduce greenhouse emissions. This should be done by the auto industry itself, as a Strategic Plan both to stay in business and as good citizens. Since 1985, U.S. Congress and the Department of Energy have been incapable of taking corrective action because of special interest pressures.

To sum up energy prospects in the United States, it is best to first define the current situation.

> On Earth Day, April 20, 2010 Americans were about to experience the largest oil spill ever to occur in the U.S. The BP oilrig exploded in the Gulf of Mexico. Environmentalists felt the oil spill would be a wake-up call to American's gluttonous consumption of oil, but in eight month's, time all appears to have been forgotten. (**Time** magazine, 12/10/10)

THE SUPPLY / DEMAND PROBLEM

Demand and price for oil fluctuates according to its perceived supply increase or decrease. Of course, as oil supply tightens, fuel prices rise. In April, 2011, gasoline prices jumped to over $4 per gallon in the United States for the first time since 2008. The rise in fuel prices is occurring because of the greater number and usage of automobiles by the middle class of both India and China.

John Hofmeister, retired former Shell Oil President, has written a book called *Why We Hate the Oil Companies*. Hofmeister predicted in December, 2010, that $5-a-gallon gasoline in the United States would become a reality by the end of 2011. Why? Because the world is using more oil.

Not to mention the U.S. dollar seems to be dropping in value every day. **The U.S. dollar lost 11% of its value in 2010.**

The United States has no national energy policy and that will continue until a person of leadership is installed who wants to do the right thing. Short supply (long gas lines) and high fuel prices could again become the burden of the American consumer in the near future.

WHY THE PROBLEM NEEDS TO BE SOLVED

Canada and Mexico, in that order, are the largest suppliers of oil to the United States. Nigeria is our number three supplier. Saudi Arabia is number four, but the Organization of the Petroleum Exporting Countries (OPEC) sets the world's selling price for selling oil.[1] The OPEC countries provide 43% of the world's oil supply, therefore OPEC is the 800-pound gorilla in the room and has the power to set the price of oil, along with speculators. OPEC was formed in September 1960, and at the present time has twelve member countries.

The perception of the American public is that a reduction of oil consumption in the United States and around the world could ease OPEC's control of the supply and price. Wrong! I feel that in the future, OPEC will reduce the production of oil to maintain high prices. When oil was priced

at over $100 a barrel, producers became addicted to money and nothing will change—besides, they know their oil fields have a finite oil capacity. Why price a finite resource cheaply?

---

1 When most of our oil comes from non-Middle East producers, one has to wonder why the U.S. military has such a presence in the Middle East. My original thought was that the U.S. military was stationed in the Middle East to keep oil prices from rising, that way other oil producers like Canada and Mexico can't raise their prices to go over par.

Meanwhile, the only immediate (and enduring) cost reduction for the American consumer will occur by curtailing their own oil consumption. It's just that simple.

WHAT IS OIL?

Oil is the residual remains of largely algae and single-celled microorganisms that lived many millions of years ago. Covered by layers of sand and mud, the heat and pressure turned the remains into giant pools of oil, called reservoirs. When oil is in the range of one to four carbon atoms, the structure takes on methane gas and turns to what is commonly referred to as dry natural gas. Taking on five to twenty carbon atoms provides the molecular structure to support heavier liquid petroleum molecules. What evolves is crude oil, which usually has a strong odor due to sulfur content, and varies in color from dark yellow to black.

Oil was originally collected from natural seeps, and for more than 35 centuries, man has put oil into lamps and used it to cook, for medicine and as a lubricant. The Chinese drilled the first known oil well in 347 A.D.

It was the invention of the automobile, particularly in the U.S., that first required vast quantities of petroleum products: from greases, to engine and transmission lubricants, to oils and fuels.

The word petroleum comes from two Latin words, *petra*, which means rock, and *oleum*, which means oil: "oil rock" or "oil of the earth." Petroleum is a general term used to define any oil-based material.

Petroleum is found in reservoirs at every level, from the Earth's surface to as deep as 15,000 feet, nearly 3 miles down.

WHAT IS CARBON?

Earth receives energy from our sun in the form of both light and heat given off in the process of a nuclear reaction between hydrogen and helium. Our sun is the center of our solar system and makes up 99.8% of our solar system's mass. The sun has about 200,000 times more mass than Earth, and is about 4.5 billion years old. Without the sun, life on Earth would not exist, but the sun could and would exist without Earth.

Energy gained from sun-produced products like wood, oil, and natural gas are all carbon-based. In fact, every living thing on Earth is carbon-based. All living things can be defined in the form of its carbon, hydrogen, oxygen, and nitrogen composition—basic biochemistry. It does not matter if we are talking about the human body, trees, plants, animals, food, or the many derivatives, such as fuel and plastics—it's all carbon based.

Everyone in the world uses carbon-based products for food, clothing, transportation, and shelter on a regular basis. Hydrocarbons are an integral part of our daily life.

CO2 in the Atmosphere

Concerned geologists and other scientists have warned the public for years regarding the finite nature of oil and other resources commonly taken for granted. Added to that is the insurmountable problem of carbon dioxides that at an alarming rate continue to build in Earth's atmosphere. The rate at which humankind has contributed to the pollution of Earth during the industrial age has done undeniable damage to the prospects of our long-term existence.

The internal combustion engine propels most of the world's 600 million vehicles. Almost all of them consume petroleum and release CO_2. Every 20-gallon tank of gasoline burned sends about 380 pounds of CO_2 into the atmosphere. These gases will hang around for an average of 100 years. The carbon dioxide that accumulates works against the natural chemistry of Earth's atmosphere, becoming a heat-absorbing blanket that envelopes us and creates global warming.

OIL CONSUMPTION

In 2006, the world used more than 85 million barrels of oil a day. In 2010, that figure was about the same, and U.S. consumption was down from 20 million barrels to 19.6 million barrels per day. On May 13, 2011, NBC News stated that the U.S. was using 19 million barrels of oil a day. The United States has less than 5% of the world's population, but consumes about 23% of the world's energy. That also means we produce more than our share of pollution and greenhouse gasses.

Today, more than 40% of the world's oil goes to fuel automobiles. In the United States, automobiles burn more than 65% of all oil consumed, and we drive more than 2.7 trillion miles each year: a distance equivalent to 10 million trips to the moon. On average, American vehicles consume 600 gallons of fuel each year and there are more than 232 million registered vehicles in the United States, more than one for every registered American with a driver's license. We are clearly the culture most addicted to oil.

The military consumes about 2% of our nation's energy. To put things into better perspective, a large Navy ship burns a gallon of fuel for every five feet it moves. Today, all eleven U.S. aircraft carriers are nuclear powered, but when they used a petroleum fuel, it took a gallon of fuel to move the carrier forward six inches. Ironically, the majority of the fuel consumed by the military goes to propel jets.

China continues as the second largest consumer of petroleum in the world, and the demand everywhere in Asia is escalating dramatically. As demand rises, the emerging nations' economies will falter as the cost per barrel soars past the high of $138, achieved June 6, 2008.

But it's our problem to quell our appetite for oil. When gasoline advances to $5 or $6 dollars per gallon, we're likely to find ourselves in another recession or depression. With the large numbers of Americans who drive SUVs, expending $150 or more each week to fill up their tanks just to get to work, a drastic drawback in spending on other daily goods could send the economy into a tailspin.

HOW THE OIL MARKET WORKS

Oil is bought and sold as futures in the commodities market in 1,000-barrel units. The price of a barrel of oil is based on the greatest refining capacity for gasoline.

West Texas Intermediate crude oil (Texas Tea) remains the prime benchmark for pricing oil worldwide. Oil that is low in viscosity, one that flows easily, is called light crude oil. Oil with low sulfur content is called a sweet crude oil. The West Texas Intermediate is a light, sweet crude oil. West Texas Intermediate oil brings more dollars per barrel than the Brent Oils from Northwest Europe, and $2 to $4 more than the OPEC oils. What is called sour crude oil has a high sulfur content that requires a more arduous refining process. OPEC oils (mostly from the Middle East) are of the sour crude variety.

A barrel of today's oil is 42 gallons, based on the volume of wooden barrels of the late 1800s. In 1861, the first shipment of a barrel of oil from the United States went to London in a 42-gallon wooden barrel. Crude oil is shipped in bulk, but continues to be counted by the barrel. In 2008, it costs about $2 per barrel to ship oil aboard a supertanker to anywhere in the world.

OIL TRANSPORTATION BY TANKER

The majority of our oil comes to the United States via pipeline from Canada or Mexico, with the rest arriving aboard supertankers.

In the 1950s, the largest oil tanker carried about 50,000 tons, or 29,700 barrels of oil, the equivalent of 12.5 million gallons of fuel. Oil transporters of the day relied on the Suez Canal for the shortest route to U.S. markets. The size of the canal determined the widths and depths of merchant vessels. In the seven years the Suez Canal was closed after the 1967 Seven Day War between Israel and Egypt, oil tankers increased in size to navigate around the Horn of Africa.

It was the reaction to the Exxon Valdez spill that led the U.S. Congress to pass the Oil Pollution Act of 1990. The law calls for any ship in U.S. water to be double-hulled by 2015. Double-hull tankers fill the space between the hulls with a mix of inert gases—like nitrogen or CO_2—to guard against a flash fire.

The efficiency of shipping in supertankers keeps the costs down, resulting in a typical accounting cost of about $.05 USD per gallon of gasoline at the pump. This remains true only if the U.S. doesn't alter its current consumption rate.

The amount of oil aboard that one ship 1950s would fuel American motorists for less than a day. In the near future, the energy needs in our country could necessitate hundreds of fully loaded supertankers each year, along with pipeline oil shipments from Canada and Mexico.

PIPELINES

The United States—and any developed nation in the world—is interlaced with pipelines. Pipelines are designed to move large quantities of commodities, like oil, natural gas, and products such as gasoline, propane, and ethylene cost effectively and in a timely manner.

A variety of oils are shipped through the same pipeline. When one type of oil is exchanged for another, there is a volume of fluids where the two products have intermixed. This slug of fuel material is of unknown quality and is called contaminated fuel. Contaminated fuels, because of their initial origination and quality, are sold at a very low price to whomever will take them.

Jim Louis of UPS and Jim Cote of General Motors teamed up to develop a small engine that would burn contaminated fuels in UPS delivery trucks. The goal of using a low-cost fuel fit under that old adage, "Waste Not, Want Not."

Natural gas is distributed around the nation by pipeline directly into the consumer's home. Some of the main distribution arteries for natural gas are 4 feet in diameter and under great pressure. Some plastic companies that make polypropylene locate their manufacturing operations adjacent to major natural gas pipeline arteries to capture raw material. Nearly half a million miles of oil and gas transmission pipeline crisscross the United States. These pipelines are integral to U.S. energy supplies and have vital links to other critical infrastructure, such as power plants, airports, and military bases.

In 2006 Congress passed the Pipeline Safety Improvement Act to improve pipeline safety and security practices, and to reauthorize the Federal Office of Pipeline Safety. In 2007, Congress passed the Implementing Recommendations of the 9/11 Commission Act of 2007. Provisions in this act mandate pipeline security inspections and potential enforcement, and require federal plans for critical pipeline security and incident recovery. Congress is overseeing the implementation of these acts and examining ongoing policy issues related to the nation's pipeline network.

WHAT IS PEAK OIL?

Peak oil is a term developed in 1969 by Shell Oil geologist M. King Hubbert. He used a bell-shaped curve to predict a schedule for when the world's oil production capacity, based on known reserves, would reach its height and set course on an unstoppable downward slope. With increased technology and the discovery of new oil fields, the bell curve has moved ahead in time.

The world consumes more than 80 million barrels of oil each day. That equates to about 29.2 billion barrels of oil each year. The United States is well beyond its domestic peak oil production, and today imports almost 60% of what it consumes. Many geologists claim that planet Earth has additional captive oil, but it will be much more difficult to access.

THE BREAKDOWN OF A BARREL OF OIL

In the United States, about 35 gallons of a 42-gallon barrel will be used for transportation fuel. Non-petroleum based additives account for approximately two gallons per barrel. On average, a barrel of OPEC oil yields about 37 gallons of transportation fuel. That breaks down to 19.6 gallons of gasoline, 7 gallons of diesel, and 7.4 gallons of kerosene and jet fuel. The remaining 7 gallons in the barrel are heaver oils, greases and tars.

OIL SPECULATION

Many oil experts feel speculation by large-scale traders in the oil commodities market have over-projected needs, even though the demand from India and China increased 12% last year. However, if the United States has an especially cold winter, Americans increase their driving habits, and if there is a terror event, the price of oil could again rise to over $130 per barrel. As of the printing of this book, oil trade prices were established with the U.S. dollar as the Worlds Reserve Currency in mind. If oil pricing and trading turns its focus to the value of another currency as a World Reserve Currency, the stability of the dollar is at great risk. The dollar's value has continued to decline because of the federal government's escalating eagerness to borrow and print money.

FIVE FACTORS THAT CONTROL OIL

The five major factors that will affect the supply of oil to the United States are extreme weather, refining capacity, oil embargoes, war, and terrorism.

- **Weather.** In the summer of 2005, the United States experienced a Category 4 hurricane that not only crippled the nation's oil production, but also brought attention to the domestic oil industry's limited refining capacity. Unforeseen catastrophic weather will continue to affect and disrupt oil production around the globe at various times each year. Extreme weather conditions or catastrophes are unpredictable, and development of automotive fuel plans should account for these situations with the worst-case scenarios in mind.

- **Refining Capacity.** For the last 20 years, the United States has had a refining capacity problem. There have been no new refineries built in the last 30 years. In 2006, British Petroleum (BP) announced it has entered the final planning stage of a $3 billion dollar investment in Canadian heavy crude oil processing by upgrading its Whiting Refinery located in Whiting, Indiana. When the plant is completed sometime in late 2011, BP will have the capacity of an additional 1.7 million gallons of gasoline and diesel fuel per day. Hopefully this will help ease the refining situation in the United States.

- **War or Revolution.** War or a revolution in an oil-supplying nation could cause a sudden jump in the price of oil. For example, Nigeria is an African country in a near-constant state of unrest. It also is the 12th largest oil exporter in the world, and one of the prime sources of oil for the United States. Any significant amount of unrest in the country would disrupt Nigeria's flow of oil to the United States and create a drastic spike in cost to already surging fuel prices. At this writing, some Middle Eastern OPEC Nations could experience protest movements by rebel factions within their countries.

- **Terrorism.** In the Middle East, there are nations other than Afghanistan, Iraq and Pakistan that are subject to the threat of al Qaeda terrorist activity. Saudi Arabia is a prime candidate for revolution. It appears to be al Qaeda's desire, as part of an overriding goal to disrupt the flow of oil to the United States, to overthrow the Saudi Government. In time I believe this will happen.

OPEC 1973 OIL EMBARGO

OPEC is a 51-year-old cartel made up of 12 developing countries. The oil embargo of 1973 refers to when OPEC raised the price of oil to be on par with the actual value of the U.S. Trade Dollar (World Reserve Currency), not wheat. Then, OPEC raised the price of oil whenever the value of the U.S. dollar began to depreciate. This was done because the Middle Eastern nations realized the value of a barrel of oil was on the decline because of the devaluation of the dollar. In 1979, with the downfall of the Shah of Iran, OPEC realized its full ability to press its will on the West with the pricing and supply of oil.

In 1973 and 1974, the American public was subject for the first time to gasoline shortages provided by the courtesy of OPEC. Sometimes the shortages were so bad, the station attendant would only allow 10 gallons per customer. Many times Americans waited in a line that sometimes wrapped around the block.

By 1981, OPEC had flexed its muscles too much and U.S. consumers answered by driving less and opting to buy more fuel-efficient vehicles. The federal government also initiated and funded alternate fuel programs.

With the increase in sales of higher-mileage vehicles, the consumption of oil began to diminish. OPEC responded with a quick change of course and rapidly dropped the price of oil to compete with emerging products, such as ethanol.

OPEC CONTROLS THE WORLD AUTO INDUSTRY

The Detroit Big Three auto companies have been brought to their collective knees many times by OPEC and oil speculator's manipulation of prices and supply. OPEC has provided some memorable and damaging effects on the cost of fuel sold to the American consumer.

Big oil companies are very cozy with U.S. Congress, made evident by the fall of prices immediately preceding the November, 2006, midterm elections. The support for alternative fuel programs brought before Congress also had what many believe is more than coincidental timing for steep and rapid reductions in the price of oil. Such maneuvers have worked well in the past to quell interest in subsidies for progressive alternative fuel programs.

Domestic automakers are now bringing new offerings for fuel-efficient vehicles, and the unrelenting stronghold of erratic oil prices on the American consumer could finally end.

BRAZIL IS VIRTUALLY FREE OF OPEC

In the early 1980s, Brazil set up a National Strategic Fuel Strategy to free itself from OPEC control. The country's goal was accomplished, and today Brazil's ethanol program serves as an example of an environmentally friendly source of fuel. The country generates the fuel with its abundance of sugar cane, which is four times more efficient than typical grain in making ethanol. Brazil even exports ethanol today.

FUTURE GOAL FOR THE U.S. MILITARY—ONE FUEL

To improve fuel efficiency, the U.S. military is trying to use one fuel for all its vehicles: jeeps, heavy trucks, tanks, aircraft and ships. The attraction of having only a single fuel to manage all the possibilities that weave together a military operation will simplify military field operations. Some factors, such as cost, availability, practicability and applicability must be taken into account on deciding what type of fuel should be used in war.

THE BRYANT BILL

Congressmen Richard Bryant and Slade Gordon endorsed fuel economy and introduced legislation to force a 40 mile-per-gallon (mpg) standard for Corporate Average Fuel Economy, or what is widely known as the CAFE standard in 1990. This was to be applicable to all vehicles sold in the United States in a ten-year ramp-up. The Bryant Bill would have required all vehicles sold in the United States to achieve a 40 mpg average among all the vehicles in their fleet. The 1975 CAFE Standard of 27.5 mpg had already been in place for 15 years when the Bryan Bill was introduced.

Something to ponder: the actual cost of the fuel American taxpayers put in their vehicles is well beyond $5 per gallon if the expenses associated with the U.S. military enter the equation.

General Motors and other automakers appeared at the hearing and testified that the new standards would add burdensome expenses that would be passed along to the consumer as a higher sticker price. Through mutual distrust, it was decided by Congress that presentations should be given to National Academy of Science for a more accurate evaluation. The President of General Motors gave the presentation to the National Academy of Science. The GM report was designed and brought forward by a team of top corporate executives. I was the lowest ranking executive on that team. The report asserted that the company would incur billions of dollars in engineering and manufacturing costs atop the recent costs of the already mandated safety standards. Ford and Chrysler chief executives gave similar presentations. Congress turned down the 40 mpg CAFE Bryon Bill. (Current CAFE rules required the halfhearted standard of 27.5 mpg in 2010 that is to be increased to 35.5 mpg by 2016.)

The U.S. auto industry has made major strides in quality during the last decade, but they are far overshadowed by the Big Three's failure to retool and move away from large, inefficient vehicles. I feel that had the

Bryant Bill of 1990 been passed to law, the American auto industry would now have an adequate mix of cars in production today that would meet the driving public's needs.

The Real Cost of the Bryant Bill

The U.S. consumer has spent billions of dollars in higher oil prices to OPEC and the other oil producers around the world. If the Bryon Bill had been enacted, those dollars would have been spent on technology right here in America, and all of America would have benefited. Hindsight is always 20/20.

To me, the Big Three actually cut their own throats by blocking the Bryant Bill. Foreign competitors were focused on sales in their domestic markets, where they were also experiencing relatively high fuel prices. They already had smaller and more economic vehicles that reflected the needs of their customers. The needs of foreign makers' customers at the time, particularly in Asia, now reflect the needs of customers in North America—thus the foreign competition was able to respond quickly and grab additional market share each time fuel prices rose.

On December 27, 2006, a key GM executive expressed similar concerns. He said General Motors would have to suspend the manufacture of full-size pick-up trucks because the company was unable to meet the longtime CAFE standard of 27.5 miles. He reasoned that it was the U.S. government that was forcing the world's largest auto maker from the large truck segment and leaving it for Toyota, who was cashing in on its breadth of fuel economy credits earned from the manufacture of so many small, fuel efficient vehicles.

AMERICA'S AUTO INDUSTRY NEEDS A STRATEGIC PLAN

Over the last 35 years, the American auto industry has had a responsibility to develop their respective Strategic Plans, plans that would deal with fuel supply and emission contingencies. Based upon corporate history, the Detroit automakers have been caught off guard every time a disruption in the fuel supply occurred, and stock values have reflected as much. It appears America's auto industries have failed to build, or at least failed to implement, strategic plans that account for the possible changes in supply and demand for fuel.

We live in a world of constant turmoil, and many factors affect the uniform flow of oil. Only when the American auto industry adopts a Strategic Plan for vehicle design requirements based on fuel cost and availability will the nature of fuel price shock will be taken into consideration.

The U.S. auto industry must become PRO-ACTIVE. It must take the lead and become the pivotal industry to make change and set fuel economy and clean air policy. Why not lead the U.S. in environmental change rather than coming along as usual, kicking and screaming like undisciplined children?

TRANSPORTATION AND THE FUTURE

Our country will be invincible if all of our 1.3 billion people can think independently and be creative. —Wen Jiaboa, Premier of China[1]

Technology is changing so fast that the world is now on a Two-Year Technological Jump. What that means is that the world is able to develop equivalent new technology in just two years. In the 1970s, the world was on a Seven-Year Technological Jump, a statistic proclaimed by GM strategic planner, James K. Paisley.

By shortening the Jump to two years, the rate of technical breakthroughs will be mind-blowing, and will surely challenge our education system. It has been projected that when a student enters college, the courses taken in the first two years could be obsolete before graduation. If this is the world we are living in today, think of what the pace of the world will be for our grandchildren! It will be madding by our standards, but the human mind and body have the ability to adapt. It's that old Darwinian theory— all plants or animals on planet Earth either adapt or die. Grandparents feel that the next generation will be able to cope and adjust to a rapidly changing environment, just as we did.

---

1 *Time* magazine - quote of the day 4/29/11.

In order to develop and project future transportation technology, it is best to have a little perspective on how fast things can change.

ROAD SYSTEMS

For most of the time that man has been on Earth, he has used pathways and trails carved into the landscape by animal herds.

It was not until the Romans built their vast empire that the need for a functioning transportation system to control and move armies and commerce came into play. Their technology for building roads and bridges has been improved upon and passed down through the ages, as the model to copy. Roman roads were so well constructed that several small segments are still being used today.

RAILROADS

In the early part of the 1880s, U.S. routes for tracks were determined by town location and business destinations in the East. With time, railroads became interlaced all across the country, from sea to shining sea. The railroad was the only major mechanical method of ground transportation before the invention of the car.

Over the years, American railroads are still using a rail system that was invented over 150 years ago. Passenger traffic on railroads was lost to the advent of jet aircraft. Rail traffic is nowadays mostly confined to hauling freight.

HIGHWAYS

Most cities in the United States had dirt-covered streets in 1900. All homes and business were serviced by horse-drawn wagons. Pavement was unnecessary as horses need soft ground for traction. To this day, the Kentucky Derby is still run on a dirt track, not asphalt.

As the nation grew into the 20th century, the demand for an improved road system evolved around the growth of automobile production. As more and more automobiles plied city streets, the narrow tires and mud from inclement weather made driving uncomfortable, and often next to impossible.

During the first 50 years of the last century, the American road system was developed in a haphazard fashion. Driving from one state to the next was an adventure that fostered many small-town tourist rest stops, featuring mini-cabins. Life traveled at a much slower pace at that time, and so did the family car. There were very few roads in America that were designed for speeds greater than 60 mph.

The topic of the 1939 World's Fair held in Flushing Meadows, New York, was "The Future." General Motors, Ford, and Chrysler were all grouped together in the transportation area. The General Motors "Futurama Exhibit" captured the most attention and was the most visited exhibit at the fair. Visionaries from GM Styling developed a "City of Tomorrow" with sweeping expressway cloverleafs and glass-covered elevated walkways between buildings. Visitors to the exhibit sat in moving chairs and wondered at future American cities connected by express highways from coast to coast. The "City of Tomorrow," with its elevated, covered walkways, made an indelible impression on everyone that saw it. Everything predicted in the 1939 exhibit became commonplace by the end of the century.

The first Interstate, the Pennsylvania Turnpike, was built during the Great Depression, but it was Dwight David Eisenhower, the 34th President of the United States, who truly revolutionized travel in the U.S. when he initiated in 1956 the bill that authorized the National Defense Highway Transportation Act. The idea arose from Eisenhower's experience in Europe during World War II.

In the mid-1930s, the world was informed that Germany's dictator, Adolph Hitler, had authorized the construction of the highway system for "the people's car." It was very similar to the Roman plan. The Autobahn was the world's first superhighway for the German people and their new car called the Volkswagen (German for *people's car*). In actuality, the Autobahn was constructed as a guise: it was really designed for the rapid deployment of troops around Germany, and built to withstand the load of heavy military vehicles. In the spring of 1945, the Autobahn also served as an airstrip for a few of the German jet aircraft Messerschmitt ME 262s.

Germany's ability to move troops from one end of the country to the other on a moment's notice convinced President Eisenhower that America also needed a national highway network. The Interstate Highway System we have today is not only because of Eisenhower's vision, but his ability to act on what needed to be done for the American driving public.

Since the inception of the National Defense Highway Transportation Act, however, providing and maintaining a functional road system for the automobile is way behind the need. Today, because of the high military budget, the United States' network of roads is now at least 20 years behind the times. It's all just a simple matter of priorities and funding. Many people in the United States sit for hours in traffic each day as a direct result of this country not addressing transportation issues properly. Implementation of new road surfaces to meet the ever-increasing demand of the driving public has always lagged behind demand.

But spending billions of dollars developing a new parallel highway system that expands the existing system might not be the most effective transportation system available. Technology is changing very fast as we enter the information age. For example, China has very few hard-wired telephone lines because the cellphone has completely circumvented the need for landlines in most applications. The same could be true for the American transportation system, as communication systems lessen the need to travel. There has to be an elegant way to upgrade our personal and mass transportation system as one.

MASS TRANSIT

When it comes to mass transit, the United States has been left in the dust, and is at least four decades behind.

Mass transit is the concept of moving large amounts of people easily from one place to another. Sounds difficult, and sometimes it is because it's all about personal space. If people can travel with enough space between them, they feel more at ease. Open space between passengers in India, Japan, or China would be still considered cramped by western standards. It's all a matter of the local perception of space.

Mass transit studies were conducted by the various American auto manufactures in the 1960s, but as an idea of how it relates to the individual, the vehicle, and commerce, it has never been fully explored here. Part of the problem is that researchers felt Americans would turn up their noses at the notion of using any conveyance system labeled "Mass Transit." Yes, some Americans ride the "L" in Chicago, the "MTA" in Boston; others ride "BART" in San Francisco, and of course the New York Subway System in New York City. Why? Because there is no place to park your frigging car, that's WHY! The New York Subway was put in during the 1890–1920 era, and autos were not a factor at that time—but they are now. In 2006, the

Hydrofoil Boat

I guess I can say my career has come full circle with this discussion: in 1960, while working with the GM Styling Research Studio, I participated in some mass transit projects. Above is one of my sketches, made in 1960, of a hydrofoil mass transit boat designed to move people around the waterways from New York City to adjacent cities in New Jersey. This concept was proposed as a means of transportation for the 1964–5 World's Fair held in Flushing Meadows Park, New York. Even though I like personal transportation, I did enjoying working on mass transportation projects.

U.S. had about 240 million licensed drivers. Of course, that number did not include the illegals driving on our roads.

Let's take a look at how other countries around the world have managed their mass public transportation.

Japan's wealth accumulated rapidly in the last four decades because they became a major economic powerhouse building high quality electronic products and automobiles. Instead of protecting the world's oil supply and playing global peace-maker, Japan invested their newfound wealth in high-speed trains. Even so, back in the late 1970s Japan was the first nation to develop and use high-speed Bullet Trains traveling over 150 mph. Japan has continued to upgrade their mass transit system so it is faster and more convenient to take the Bullet Train than it is to fly.

China has over 1,700 kilometers of high-speed rail lines. China has taken one of the their newest Bullet Trains, designed to travel at 250 mph, and placed it between Beijing and Shanghai, a distance of about 300 miles. With those speeds and the traffic congestion in China, the route will become the obvious choice for travelers. Someday Cargo Bullet Trains will be added to passenger high-speed trains as a method of improving cargo transportation efficiency, but it can also lead to a reduction in fares for passengers.

Germany, France and Spain all have high-speed rail systems today. Some could say for that progressive countries dealing with confined spaces and high populations, high-speed rail is the only choice.

The United States planning people need to rethink the over-all mass transportation process by considering moving people, their vehicles, and commerce all around the country using a single integrated system.

The United States has a very unused railroad right-of-way system that is totally suitable for a dual transportation system. The Eastern corridor is actually an ideal place for high-speed rail because of high population

I had the opportunity to travel by a Bullet Train to Nagoya at the base of Mount Fuji for a meeting with a Japanese automobile manu-facturer. The ride was impres-sive, and we were told by our handler that when the train stopped, we should exit the door, step out ten feet, turn left and walk ten feet—a bald fat man would be greeting us. We followed instructions and met a fellow bowing before us who had more hair than my engineering buddy and was lighter in weight than myself. I jokingly asked my fellow engineer, **How do you think he describes us?**

density and short distances between major cities. A new mass transit system, fully capable of servicing the individual, their vehicles, and the shipping commerce is totally feasible by using the overhead right-of-way on existing rail road tracks, coupled to the interstate highway system. This would be the lowest cost approach to a Mass Transit System that could serve everyone.

Mass transportation for personal and vehicle usage should be priced low to encourage full utilization of the system. Charges to use Mass Transit should be priced well below the cost of personal vehicle to entice customers.

This is a golden opportunity for the proposed Ford and GM Design and Engineering Group merger. They could design a lease vehicle that could be packaged and easily transferred to high-speed trains for shipping. The vehicle needs to carry luggage and be designed as a vehicle of convenience, once the passenger and vehicle have reached their desired destination. Innovations like this are greatly needed in the next 20 years as more and more people living in the United States reach retirement age. Also, this Mass Transit project would create many new jobs for Americans citizens.

MAGLEV RAPID TRANSIT SYSTEM

A Maglev transportation system uses magnetic levitation for lift and propulsion of the vehicle. Maglev is quiet, smooth, and much faster than any high-speed train with wheels. Most of the electrical energy required to propel the Maglev vehicle is used to move the air around the vehicle. The power requirement just to move the air at 350 mph has to be over 90% of the total energy used.

The Shanghai Maglev Train in China is known for its technology and is in use every day transporting passenger the 19 miles to the Shanghai airport in about 8 minutes at speeds up to 250 mph. The Shanghai Maglev Train is definitely a sign of things to come in the 21st century.

TELEMATICS

The automotive industry's long association with advanced technology continues to see a bright future rising above the horizon. The 21st century is rapidly proving itself to be the computer and information age. The automotive industry must embrace this age, and adopt business models that continue to lead the way in automotive electronics and telecommunication integration. This rapidly changing field has come to be known as telematics, and it is revolutionizing the mobile communications and automotive industries. Today, the telematics-equipped vehicle is mostly known as a cellphone enabler.

> Telematics offer a unique and intimate buying experience for the future consumer where they truly become one (integrated) with their vehicle.

Today the automobile is able to recognize the driver, adjust the seat and mirrors, park, and automatically detect a cellphone or personalized digital assistant (PDA). Future telematics systems must employ a greater interactive system with the vehicle owner. To remain innovative, future systems must provide a cohesive environment between the manufacturer and owner. As technology advances into the 21st century, interactive-based systems such as telematics can reinstall confidence in the American automotive industry.

New telematics are being introduced to promote personal safety. Global Life Line, a California company, has developed a safe key fob with a button that will automatically notify the police and give your GPS posi-tion even when outside and away from the vehicle. The rational was that people always carry their car keys.

NEW ALTERNATIVE ENERGY

I believe that the great Creator has put ores and oil on this earth to give us a breathing spell. As we exhaust them, we must be prepared to fall back on our farms, which is God's true storehouse and can never be exhausted. We can learn to synthesize material for every human need from things that grow.
—George Washington Carver

Almost everything that involved the American automobile for the last 100 years has used oil as the fuel of power. There are many alternate energy sources that can be considered, and they have been included in this chapter.

WHAT IS THE PROBLEM?

The long and short of it that is that oil supplies are getting shorter and more costly, and their use is polluting the planet with greenhouse gases. Adapting other sources of energy need to be developed to power both the internal combustion engine (ICE) and the many new electrical vehicles proposed in the future.

WHY THE PROBLEM NEEDS TO BE SOLVED, AND WHAT ARE THE IMPLICATIONS?

When the worlds' automotive manufacturers offer more fuel-efficient vehicles, there will be a reduction in NOX and CO_2 gases. Any new alternate fuel source that is cleaner and in the same cost range as oil will be perceived as a technical break-through.

HOW TO SOLVE THE PROBLEM AND ARRIVE AT A PLAUSIBLE SOLUTION

Both Ford and General Motors need to establish a Strategic Plan that encompasses a Strategic Energy Plan to better understand the control of the energy supply and how to react to it. These last, two American auto companies also need to set some clear-cut goals to improve vehicle fuel economy to the 50 mpg range, thus reducing greenhouse emissions. More importantly, alternate energy sources offer an opportunity to provide pollution-free transportation. The last, two true American auto companies should take the lead in setting a clean air policy for the nation.

Let's look at some of these alternatives.

NATURAL RESOURCES

- **Enhanced Oil Recovery.** Enhanced Oil Recovery (EOR) is an unconventional way to recover additional oil from exhausted and depleted fields by using CO_2. A typical oil field only yields 20–40% of the original find, with most of the oil remaining in pockets. By injecting CO_2 into the well, most of the remaining oil is forced to existing well pumps. EOR, is projected to recover between 20–50% of the original find.

- **Natural gas.** Natural gas, also known as methane gas, is a simple one-carbon molecular structure (CH4) and provides nearly complete combustion. Demand for natural gas is high because it's a clean-burning alternative to coal or petroleum for home heating, and is also useful in electrical generation facilities.

- **Compressed natural gas.** Compressed natural gas (CNG) is simply natural gas stored under pressure in cylinders for use as a fuel source. If just 5% of all new vehicles manufactured by the American auto industry converted to CNG by 2014, the effect would be a dramatic reduction in the need for foreign oil. Also, there is a notable reduction in CO2 with the use of CNG.

- **Liquefied natural gas.** Liquefied natural gas (LNG) is natural gas that has been compressed using high pressures, then condensed by cooling. LNG occupies about 1/614 the volume of natural gas, and is used for bulk shipping.

- **Liquid petroleum gas.** Liquid petroleum gas (LPG), or propane, is a byproduct of the crude oil finishing process. It can also be extracted from oil or gas streams as they emerge from the ground. LPG will evaporate at normal temperatures.

- **Coal.** The United States, Russia, and China have the world's largest coal reserves, in that order. The U.S. has vast reserves of coal that are going to last for many centuries to come. Cheap coal was the energy source that fundamentally started the industrial revolution.

- **Liquefied coal.** In the late 1920s, Nazi Germany successfully synthesized a liquid diesel fuel from coal. The liquefaction of coal is called the Fischer –Tropsch Process.

- **Methanol.** A cleaner burning fuel is derived when methanol is added to conventional gasoline. The combining of 85% methanol to 15%

gasoline could be offered here in the United States as M-85, for internal combustion engine use.

- **Synthetic natural gas.** Synthetic natural gas (SNG) can also be manufactured from coal, although some oil people say, "Synthetic natural gas is an oxymoron." Nonetheless, the reaction in the formation of SNG is an initial step in the manufacture of other coal products.

> The U.S. military is encouraging the development and production of a high performance alternative fuel for its applications. The military goal is to secure 50% of aviation fuel from domestic alternative sources by 2018.

- **Oil shale.** It has been said that the United States has about 75% of all of the oil shale in the world, or the equivalent of 1.6 trillion barrels oil. Extracting oil from the shale is no simple task, but the conversion to oil from oil shale in quantity is, I think, less than a decade away.

- **Oil sands.** The oil sands of Alberta's Athabasca region in Canada offer the next great oil boom in North America. The Athabasca region alone has an estimated 175 billion barrels of easy-to-reach oil in the form of oil sands. Removing the tars from the oil-soaked sand involves a tremendous amount of energy, as the sand must be boiled.

- **Solar energy.** A solar/electrical unit could be placed on the roofs of motor vehicles to supply vehicle electric energy for charging the batteries and help reduce the parasitic power losses when running accessories. Solar energy is one of our greatest potential sources of clean energy, and engineers worldwide are exploring ways to provide electrical power for mankind that is totally renewable.

- **Wind energy.** Simply put, wind energy is the result of the sun heating up Earth's surface and moving the atmosphere as Earth rotates on its axis. Wind energy, like solar energy, is a renewable energy resource, and tapping into it has virtually no downside. Why not have homeowners harvest their own electrical energy for transportation? This could all happen within the next three to five years with a compact wind electrical generating machine and plugged-in electric vehicle.

- **Wave energy.** Wave power is the capture and harnessing of ocean waves and its conversion into electrical power. Capturing wave energy is just in its infancy, and the world certainly has a tremendous amount of wave energy force that is eroding our shores and beaches every day.

> For a successful technology, reality must take precedence over public relations, for nature cannot be fooled.
> —Richard Feynman, U.S. educator and physicist

- **Geothermal energy.** Geothermal energy is energy derived from Earth's internal heat. Reviewing the potential of geothermal energy, it's a wonder the United States hasn't already embarked on a focused geothermal/electric program. The potential numbers of geothermal energy are so tremendous it is hard to believe no one has taken the vast amount of energy beneath our feet seriously.

  The potential geothermal energy is estimated to be over 50,000 times all of the gas and oil resources in the world today, and it's totally pollution free. It has been pointed out that even with today's technology, the cost of producing geothermal energy in the form of steam continues to be higher than the lowest cost coal-fired steam electrical power plants. What is needed is a little Yankee Ingenuity applied to common sense to turn geothermal energy into a planet-saving environmental solution.

- **Heat pumps.** The heat pump is a mechanical device that moves heat in the form of a fluid from one location to another. For example, it can transfer heat from a house to the soil for cooling in the hot summer months, and reverse the process during the colder winter months. Heat pumps apply mostly to home applications.

- **Hydrogen.** The projected time frame for limited production of hydrogen gas (H2) will be in the third decade of the 20st century. Hydrogen-powered fuel cell vehicles are still a long way off. Many within the technical community hold this view.

- **Hydroelectric power.** The Hoover Dam is an excellent example of hydroelectric power generation. Today, the dam is the main electri-

Robert Templin, retired Chief Engineer of the Cadillac Motor Division, reported his thoughts on hydrogen and fuel cell vehicles. His article appeared in the Cadillac Club book, called **The Self Starter** (October, 2006). Mr. Templin's review is titled, "Hydrogen and Fuel Cells No Solution." He stated that based on his experience on the slow development of the hydrogen supply infrastructure, safety issues, and cost, hydrogen will not be available in the foreseeable future as an automobile fuel. Mr. Templin felt that a Prius hybrid-type vehicle will be the mainstay fuel-efficient vehicle for the next decade or two, as the auto industries sort out their various fuel efficiency options. Bob Templin passed away in 2009.

cal power source for Las Vegas. An excellent example of harnessing hydroelectric power for the benefit of man of mankind is the Tennessee Valley Authority (TVA). Started as part of the New Deal Program in 1933, the TVA has offered economic opportunity for a seven-state region ever since.

- **Stream electric power.** Water from a small stream is used to generate electrical power through a mini water turbine. The electrical output is sufficient for supplementing electrical power for the home, farm use, or the family plug-in, hybrid vehicle.

- **Nuclear power.** The nuclear electrical power industry has been dealt a few serious blows. First, the movie "China Syndrome" was a totally emotional scare about everything that could go wrong. Second, the American public had a real scare a few months after the movie's release when personnel and management blunders nearly caused a meltdown of a reactor at Three Mile Island in Pennsylvania. Thirdly, years later, the USSR Chernobyl Nuclear Breeder Reactor became the world's worst nuclear power accident. The Chernobyl nuclear reactors chain reaction explosion caused a total reactor meltdown on April 26, 1986, that has left a lasting impression of nuclear power gone amuck. Finally, the Japanese 9.0 earthquake and tsunami of March 11, 2011. In the aftermath of the disaster, many nations began to re-examine their nuclear programs. I feel that nuclear power will remain in limbo until the next decade.

BIO FUELS

Biofuels offer the United States—and actually the rest of the world—an opportunity to become more self-sufficient and free of OPEC's stranglehold. But selecting the proper biofuel technology will not be an easy process.

- **Ethanol.** Henry Ford was definitely a man ahead of his time. Ford was a strong believer in ethanol as a biofuel for the emerging auto industry of the late 1920s and early 30s, when the Ford Motor Car Company and Standard Oil of New Jersey had a functional business relationship. Surprisingly, ethanol used to account for 25% of fuel sales in the 1920s.

- **Cellulose ethanol.** Cellulose ethanol is manufactured from plant waste, including yard clippings, corn stocks, straw, even wood chips. All plant life contains cellulose, which makes it the most common organic material on the planet. The only problem is, cellulose ethanol always seems to be "just five years away from production," but it never gets there. Every five years it's still five years away, a situation

AGRO-ENERGY

Farmers are the only indispensable people on the face of the earth. **—Li Zhaoxing, Ambassador, China**

Today, the American public finds itself literally over a barrel. American automobile companies have encouraged the use of American grown corn, wheat, and other grain crops to make ethanol and other biodiesel fuels from feedstock. Why? Because for every flex-fuel vehicle manufactured, the automaker receives CAFE credits that help them offset some of their less fuel-efficient offerings. This kind of horse-trading allows them to subsidize the manufacture of what they're good at: gas-guzzling vehicles that do not meet the 1985 CAFE law.

And it isn't as if flex-fuel vehicles were all that complicated: they are very cost effective (cheap) to produce. But instead of focusing research and development in this area, the American auto industry is just using flex-fuel as a way to take advantage of the system.

So what's going on here? The reality is that agricultural seed companies and the auto industry in the United States are pushing us into becoming a nation of farmers, just like at the end of the 19th century. The more things change, the more they remain the same: we've gone full circle, from agriculture to industry, and back to agriculture.

Agro-energy will become the United States' foothold in the world economy as fossil fuels become politically unsustainable and no longer environmentally economical. Farmers could then play the critical role in providing food, renewable energy and energy security for the United States. American farmers should form a grain cartel: the Organization of Food Producing Nations (OFPN). Agriculture could become a replacement for the U.S. industrial base should we lose it.

that could go for the next 25 years as researchers search for funding for their overstated claims.

- **Biodiesel.** As the world searches for environmentally friendly alternate engines and fuel replacements, the diesel engine has been sitting right under their noses. Diesel engines can run on vegetable oil!

- **B5 & B20 biodiesel.** Over the last couple of years, the Federal Government has supported additional research into biodiesel, which is a clean-burning alternative fuel. The current national standard for biodiesel on the market today is the B5, or a 5% blend of bio-fuel with 95% petroleum diesel fuel. The U.S. government approved B20 biodiesel fuel that is 20% bio and 80% petroleum-based diesel. Any use of a blend with over 20% bio oils will require additional testing by the National Bio Diesel Board, who approves all diesel fuel blends.

- **Animal and vegetable fat diesel fuel.** As far-fetched as it may seem, human fat, a product extracted during liposuction surgery, can be rendered into oil.[1] Over 60% of Americans are overweight, and some are resorting to liposuction to reduce their body fat condition. Jackson Memorial Hospital in Florida accumulates over 11,500 liters of human fat each week. It would be much better to use the liposuction waste in a positive fashion than to discard in a landfill. As our forefathers used to say, "Waste Not, Want Not."

- **Bio natural gas.** The European nations of Sweden, Denmark, and Netherlands are all using bio natural gas to help fuel their countries' transportation needs. They are using an anaerobic digester to use all plant material, vegetable scraps, animal, and human waste to produce CH4 and CO2. The CO2 is used grow hydroponic vegetables and the CH4 becomes compressed natural gas (CNG) for transportation fuel. Driving a vehicle using bio-methane (CH4) is like being propelled down the road by flatulence.

THE ELECTRICAL GRID

Plug-in electric vehicles could utilize lithium ion batteries for a total electric vehicle, or as a plug-in/CNG hybrid vehicle. When the auto industry teams with electric power companies to provide vehicles that are eas-

---

1 Human fat is just like pig fat (lard). Animal and vegetable oil burn about the same.

ily recharged from the owner's home during non-peak periods, plug-ins could provide a viable transportation alternative.

- **Diesel/electrical energy.** In remote rural areas, electrical energy is sometimes provided by a diesel/electrical generator operation. Electrical companies will have to become a greater part of the electrical grid all across America in order to guarantee electrical energy for all of their customers that purchased plug-in hybrids.

BATTERY POWER

Battery-powered vehicles could become a predominate part of transportation in the 21st century. In the future many electric hybrid vehicles will have plug-in batteries for overnight charging. Plug-in battery hybrid vehicles will enable the driving public to capture electrical energy from power companies during the evening off-peak service hours.

- **Lead acid batteries.** The lead acid battery was invented in 1859, and still represents over 50% of all batteries manufactured today. The lead acid battery is the major use for lead in the world. Versatility of the lead acid battery to produce both high and low currents across wide temperature ranges is the main reason the batteries are so popular.

- **Ni-MH battery.** Nickel-metal hydride (Ni-MH) batteries were the second-generation batteries used in electric vehicles (EV). Nickel-metal hydride batteries have twice the energy density of lead acid batteries, at a little more than half the weight.

- **Lithium ion battery,** Lithium ion batteries are the current "in" battery because they have an excellent power density to weight ratio. In a battery applications, lithium's specific energy is up to five times greater than any lead acid battery they are replacing, due to its high electropositivity. Lithium ion batteries are also much lighter in weight, up to one fourth, while still delivering both a higher and more stable voltage profile than comparable lead acid batteries.

- **The layered battery.** Batteries have been around for over 150 years, and there is always a way to build a better mousetrap, and a better battery. Often when technology and a manufacturing process from one industry are applied to an entirely different industry, spectacular advances are made.

The technology used to build the layered battery is based on the printing process and utilizes thin metal foils and film coatings for both the positive and negative electrode plates.

The electric car people will feel they have found the Holy Grail of electric batteries when the layered battery is finally made available to the public.

FORD AND GM CAN BECOME STEWARDS OF THE PLANET

The environment is changing, we all know that. We are all witnesses to the many small changes over the years. If this were occurring 30,000 years ago, Mother Earth would tell man, "Evolve or Die." Some prominent scientists have stated, "The world may only have between 10 and 150 years until we pass the point where it will be very difficult to have a full environmental recovery within a reasonable length of time." What if the alarming message from the environmentalist is not a phony fear after all, but a reality of Earth's cyclical changes, capped by the minor role played by human beings and their con-

> Climate change is for real. We have just a small window of opportunity and it is closing rather rapidly. There is not a moment to lose.
> —Dr. Rajendra Pachauri, Chairman, Intergovernmental Panel on Climate

tribution of increased CO_2 content in the atmosphere? We may never know, but we should at least try something because Mother Earth appears to be getting overheated.

> When the earth is sick and polluted, human health is impossible....
> To heal ourselves we must heal our planet, and to heal our planet we must heal ourselves. —Bobby McLeod, Koori activist

Some people say Global Warming is happening now, others say it's just a part of Earth's climatic changes—others frankly claim we just don't know. Wouldn't it be better to err on the safe side and start taking some type of corrective action now?

An environmental image that will give both Ford and General Motors a positive glow is preserving the planet by conserving energy and reducing CO_2 emissions. In the past, automobiles have been the source of a significant amount of emissions pollution, and we recognize the need to correct the situation. The main message that Ford and GM need to project is that all of their vehicles are becoming cleaner and more fuel efficient every day, because visionary engineers are once again running the companies. When it comes to creating the Strategic Plans at Ford and General Motors, the beancounters have to be replaced with visionary technical people. The environmental image and integrity of Ford and General Motors will be greatly enhanced, when the slogan becomes: **Ford and General Motors are Living in Harmony with the Environment.**

Despite their recent turnaround, the Detroit Big Three are about to face difficult times again. There will be no room for making mediocre little decisions or taking small monetary personal sacrifices as a matter of job preservation. All three have squandered billions of dollars pussy footing around while their top executives maintained their high-living jobs, lucrative bonuses, and stock options. Innovation is needed right now, not when disaster hits. If a significant downturn in the economy occurs in 2012, as I have been projecting could happen, sales will dry up along with cash flow. When that happens, the U.S. government certainly wouldn't

BUILDING A HYBRID

Automotive engineers have long since identified and listed some known facts:

Reduced vehicle weight provides better fuel mileage
Aerodynamics improves fuel economy
Speeds above 85 mph drastically effect fuel economy, and reduce vehicle product life
A smaller engine size improves fuel economy
Short, "Stop & Go" trips greatly affect fuel economy

All of which point to the efficacy of a plug-in/(CNG) internal combustion engine hybrid vehicle:

Lighter Gross Vehicle Weight (a GVW of 2,200–2,400 Lbs.)
Reduced engine size (an ICE of 1.5 liter)
0–60 mph time (in the 9–10 second range)
125–250 mpg or better (with a plug-in hybrid and compressed natural gas (CNG) as the fuel)
Top speed (of 70–85 mph)
Totally aerodynamically designed vehicle (Cd of .250 at 7 degrees yaw)

step in again. The only sources to turn to will be investors from Asia or the Middle East, who'll be delighted to pick up the pieces for a song.

It will take good old Yankee Ingenuity, and the involvement and commitment of everyone to help Ford and General Motors become competitive again by producing vehicles that provide value to customers.

The reality of the current automotive fuel situation is: natural gas (CH4) is the only immediately available source of hydrocarbon energy capable of replacing foreign oil as a transportation fuel.

Over the course of ten years the United States could cut it's dependency on imported oil to almost nil by using natural gas (CH4). It's about time the U.S. starts looking for sensible solutions that have a direct effect on our economy.

PART FOUR: INNOVATION

YANKEE INGENUITY

THE LEASE/RECYCLE PROGRAM

YANKEE INGENUITY

Impossible is not a fact. It's an opinion — Muhammad Ali

For the last two centuries, Yankee Ingenuity has been able to build a better mousetrap and beat the competition. From Eli Whitney's cotton gin, to Thomas Edison and the light bulb, to the Wright brother's airplane. The list goes on and on. The auto industry has its own set of Yankee Ingenuity geniuses: Henry Ford, the Dodge Brothers, Ransom E. Olds, Billy Durant, Alfred P. Sloan, Henry Leland, Boss Kettering, Charlie Nash, Walter P. Chrysler, Bill Knudsen, Ed Cole ... then the list tapers off to nothing. Facing the 21st century, there appears to be a lack of can-do Yankee Ingenuity people left in the automobile industry. It has to be restored.

FORD, GM AND YANKEE INGENUITY

Getting new ideas into the Detroit Big Three system could be equated to spawning salmon; it was always an upstream battle. If you can envision an video of Alaskan salmon jumping into the open jaws of a hungry grisly bear, the salmon is the person with the idea. To me, the auto industry has become saturated with executives who are just plod mundanely through life. They rarely listen to the troops down the line who make things happen. They alone have all the answers.

> I believe in intuition and inspiration. Imagination is more important than knowledge.
> For knowledge is limited, whereas imagination embraces the entire world, stimulating progress, giving birth to evolution. It is, strictly speaking, a real factor in scientific research
> —Albert Einstein

> If necessity is the mother of invention, then competition is the father of invention.
> —Unknown

In a world where technology is moving forward at unbelievable rates, what's left of the American auto industry faces being passed by the wayside. Gone are the days of developing and selling a hot car like the 1965 Mustang. We are living in a totally new era where the expectation in the lease or purchase of a vehicle evolves many facets of the buyer's life. The Japanese and Koreans are good at understanding this, but until very recently, not so the Americans. Only now are they discovering that they can make money on small cars by including content and technology previously found only in larger models. Without moving small cars in larger volume, they will have no hope of meeting upcoming tough, federal fuel economy standards.

BRIGHT IDEA
Innovation is needed to establish a long-term, auto lease loyalty with the American public. Dealership service centers could be located next to major malls, so vehicles could be repaired while the customer shops. Some ideas may seem far-out unless they're tried out. One colleague suggests buyers might be offered X-amount of the automaker's stock FREE with every purchase to help build loyalty!

Leadership at Ford and General Motors needs to dig back to the roots of what made the American auto industry and the United States of America great. The United States is the Melting Pot of Nations. Its diverse culture and pioneering spirit spawned the expansion of the United States across this great continent. It was Yankee Ingenuity that fostered the acceleration of creativity, invention, and growth of our great nation. It was Yankee Ingenuity and creativity that allowed us to surpass all of Europe and Asia in the late-19th and 20th centuries. It has been through the efforts of creative immigrants and native sons that the United States has been able to become leaders in transportation, from railroads in the 19th century to automobiles, airplanes, and space travel in the 20th century.

Based on a 2009 study by the Information Technology and Innovation Foundation, the U.S. ranks dead-last among 40 industrialized nations in innovative competitiveness based on higher education, investment, research, and development. To survive, prosper, and develop truly American-engineered vehicles, the Detroit Three must not only stop stifling innovation, but learn to nurture ideas no matter where they come from. Innovations are needed to bring customers into dealers' showrooms, to control future material costs in a resource-short world, and to tap the creative talent of future customers.

YANKEE INGENUITY SUGGESTION PROGRAM

During World War II, all of United States industry was building equipment and munitions for the war effort. The country's manufacturing might initiated a suggestion program to get everyone's ideas, in an effort to improve the quality and production output. Some say the ideas that came pouring in helped to shorten the duration of the war by many months, or maybe years. Many say the ideas saved many American lives. The Japanese and the Germans were defeated using American resources, and a lot of effort and downright Yankee Ingenuity. America was strong, and Ford, General Motors, and the Chrysler Corporation were among the major contributors.

When Ford and General Motors Management Teams finally realize that employees are their primary resource and their most important asset, success is sure to happen. Having a motivated, creative workforce is an essential ingredient for success.

The YANKEE INGENUITY SUGGESTIONS PROGRAM is one of the quickest ways to turn Ford and General Motors around for the following reasons:

1. Employees want to rally and help their ailing company because their jobs are at stake. Employees do not intentionally come to work to screw off—they want to be productive and feel a sense of accomplishment at the end of each day. When employees are contributing to a common cause, they get a sense of pride, satisfaction, and gratification for their efforts.

2. When companies the size of Ford and General Motors are processing over $60 billion in purchased materials and paying out over $25 billion in salaries and benefits on an annual basis, there is a lot of opportunity for improvement. There is at least a potential cost savings of 5%. That is $60 + $25 billion = $85 billion in change. Take $85 billion x 5% = and that is over $4.25 billion in potential savings.

3. Today's warranty costs are in the billions of dollars each year for both GM and Ford. If a part is eliminated and the assembly is simplified and reduced in part-count, the part removed can never fail and cause a warranty problem. This is an additional plus savings in dollars and cents.

4. If a suggestion improves quality, the vehicle warranty costs are also reduced. This is an additional plus savings in dollars and cents.

5. With a serious Yankee Ingenuity Employee Suggestions Program in place, the employees would finally

feel that management has some forward vision and wants to recognize and value the creative mind, talent, and input from every employee. This is a very important factor in correcting most of Ford and GM's problems of honesty and trust.

6.   When employees are making a real contribution to improve the bottom-line for the corporation, and the management team sets real Strategic Planning Goals with a forward vision, the corporation will see real creativity. The Yankee Ingenuity Suggestions Program and the Corporate Strategic Plan then would function hand in hand.

A newly formatted Suggestion Program under proper leadership will be the first major step put trust back into the Ford and GM.

How the Old Program Works

An automobile is a summation of as many as 30,000 individual parts, assembled into components that are put together to function as a total vehicle. The Detroit Big Three employees, handling these parts and components on a daily basis, are capable of seeing how to improve the design or assembly first hand, and simplify and improve the assembly operation to make the operation function better.

All of Detroit's Automotive Big Three Employee Suggestion Programs are very similar. The following is a generic composite suggestions program.

•   A suggestion is submitted by filling out a suggestion form and depositing it in a suggestions box.

- The Suggestion Department empties the suggestions box on a regular basis. Suggestions are initially reviewed by the Suggestions Department. An acknowledgment form is sent to the person making the suggestion that it has been received and currently under evaluation.

- The suggestion is then sent to the department where the idea would apply, for evaluation.

Unfortunately, the current Employee Suggestion Programs are judged as being one of the corporations' most deceitful programs by those are eligible to use them. Most existing Employee Suggestion Programs only pay 1/6 the savings (figured on a 12-month time period from implementation) derived from the suggestion, up to a maximum payout of $20,000 for an individual, or $25,000 for a team award. All further profits belong to the company.

Employees within the Detroit Big Three consider the Employee Suggestion Programs one big joke. Opinions go downhill from there. Many employees, from all three organizations, have had suggestions turned down, only to see the idea implemented in the next major product design change.

Of course, the person responsible for the design change was also the person who reviewed the original suggestion and turned it down "because it could not be done at that time." Granted, the person reviewing suggestions is generally cramming the thankless suggestion assignment into an already stressful work schedule. Some engineers have had up to 90 suggestions stacked on their desk at one time, awaiting review. The people reviewing the suggestions are not paid any more money by their companies; it is part of their engineering work assignment. Most engineers only act on suggestions when harassed by their boss or the Suggestions Department. Then, they level the pile in a totally tasteless manor with rude remarks for rejection. Sometimes, however, in the process of reading a suggestion, an idea sticks in the subconscious mind, only to be revised and used at a later date. It is important to remember that when any idea is placed in someone else's mind and later slightly altered, it becomes the new person's idea. It's only human nature!

The current Employee Suggestion Programs at any one of the Detroit Big Three are totally abominable, and almost non-existent. The reality is, almost all of the Employee Suggestion Programs are riddled with mistrust. Employees who have turned in suggestions feel that the suggestion evaluators in the past have lied and stolen their ideas, and then cheated them out of their fair reward.

In the past years, if employees felt they had been cheated out of suggestion award money, they had the option to sue the company. Sometimes, against all odds, they won. Many more creative employees just smugly kept the ideas to themselves.

In reality, employees quit submitting suggestions because they just didn't trust their company's Employee Suggestion Program or the company people who ran it. Ideas only came from new employees because the old timers knew how the system really worked. The other reality is that the Detroit Big Three did not save much money using Employee Suggestion Programs, but the major loss was the loss of TRUST in Ford or General Motors, in the perceived process of trying to pinch pennies.

How the New Yankee Ingenuity Suggestions Program Works

The new program will revise the basic structure of the current Employee Suggestion Programs, but it will open itself up to tap the creative minds of everyone on this planet who has an IDEA and a valid driver's license.

Yankee Ingenuity Suggestion Program Implementation is a Three-Step Process:

Step 1: Any new program of this magnitude will have a few kinks and bugs that will need to get worked out. So at first, The Yankee Ingenuity Suggestion Program will only operate internally, within the two corporations. It will take between two and three months to train and inform all employees of the new corporate commitment to stand up and use good, old Yankee Ingenuity to turn the corporations around. With the full support of the corporate management teams, employees will put their hearts and souls into developing creative solutions for their corporations. It will take a good six months or more before employees realize it is an honest program with integrity.

Step 2: Open up the Yankee Ingenuity Suggestion Program to all Ford and GM retirees, component supplier employees, and dealership employees. Within this group of people lies a wealth of creative talent and years of experience. The second step will take a full six months to implement.

Step 3: Open the Yankee Ingenuity Suggestion Program to everyone on the planet with a driver's license. Suggestion forms will be available at all Ford or General Motors' dealerships. People with ideas will help increase dealership showroom traffic. The worldwide program will be initiated a full year after the initial Yankee Ingenuity program is introduced to employees.

At this point, the Chairman and the Board of Directors of both Ford and GM will open the New York Stock Exchange. They will signal a new direction for the last, two American Automobile companies by ringing the bell and introducing the Yankee Ingenuity Suggestion Program to all of Ford and GM customers—those past, present, and future.

HOW AN APPROVED EMPLOYEE SUGGESTION IS PAID OUT

When a suggestion is accepted for implementation, the following costs are summarized to establish the payout value.

- First, the engineering, tooling, and product costs to implement a suggestion are to paid off.

- Once the break-even point is established, the value of the suggestion starts generating numbers.

- Then, an employee suggestion's financial award is calculated for one year. The one-year timeframe starts the first day the suggestion is put into production.

- If the suggestion is not a production item, but still has some intrinsic value to the corporation, the suggestion committee gives an intangible award.

Let's Track the Suggestion Monies on the Old Program

An employee or team turns in a suggestion that saves the company a $1,000,000.00 over a year. That translates into a savings of over $.50 for every vehicle (2 million unit total volume, many overlapping models).

The suggested idea is used on vehicles for years, as the design cycle remains in production. The normal product design lifecycle is five to six or more years, depending on the vehicle. Savings over a five-year life-cycle would amount to $5,000,000.00. If the company paid the author $25,000.00 for the idea, then the company made the following money on the idea: (Engineering and Tooling Cost were not included because this is only an example)

$5,000,000.00 - $25,000.00 = $4,975,000.00

or the company paid only $25,000.00 / $5,000,000.00 = .005 or .05%

or 5 one-thousandth of a percent

in other words, a 199 times return on their investment.

I feel that each of Detroit's Big Three lost these kinds of savings on a daily basis because they did not understand that creative thinking is directly connected to trust.

Now Let's Look at the Suggestion Monies in the New Program

Run properly, the Yankee Ingenuity Suggestion Program involves a total I WIN, YOU WIN, WE ALL WIN mentality.

> **Win # 1:** Pay the employee/person/team 1/6 the savings, up to a maximum of $50,000 for each suggestion implemented.

> **Win # 2:** Pay the implementation engineer(s) 1/6 the savings, up to $50,000 for each idea implemented. This way the idea goes into effect immediately.

Win # 3: The corporation still makes 2/3 of the profit after the combined payout of awards ($100,000). This still amounts to $200,000 in profit on every maximum award and 100% of all savings after the initial award is paid out. Not a bad business situation, earning money while at the same time getting the work force to TRUST the company and work harder for the betterment of the corporation. It is all based on mutual interest.

The first thing the companies' top brass will say is, based on their experience, "the Yankee Ingenuity Suggestion Program will probably get abused." From my personal experience, though, I've found that when trust was placed directly on employees' shoulders, they respect that trust and work hard not to violate or abuse. Also, I believe that a program of this size will police itself—employees will want it to run properly and correctly and see that no one cheats. They will want to protect the Yankee Ingenuity Suggestion Program for everyone.

CORPORATE PUBLIC RELATIONS STAFFS

Public Relations Staff at Ford and General Motors will be delighted with the Yankee Ingenuity Suggestion Program. It has been a long time since the Public Relations Staff have had such a positive story to work with! Highlighted in the press and in soft TV advertisements, Ford and General Motors will change their integrity image overnight. Ford and GM will be portrayed as the "CAN DO" American companies, willing to open up and work with the creative minds of the American people.

The Yankee Ingenuity program will be featured in advertisements to prep the American buying public to want to participate when the program is available to them. Show Yankee Ingenuity winners on television (everyone's 15 minutes of fame) receiving checks from the company's chairman. When the American consumer sees that American autoworkers from Ford and General Motors are just like them, they will relate. It is a positive connection! The American consumers will identify with these people—Americans and their Yankee Ingenuity ideas building American transportation for them.

And, they too can become part of the creative American automotive experience and be on television. Ford and General Motors will use Yankee Ingenuity to entice the American consumer to come into dealerships and be creative. Ford and General Motors will encourage consumers through TV advertisement to come into the dealerships and submit their ideas on how to make the American cars better.

When outstanding ideas are put into production, the person with the idea will be recognized on national television. They will be given a lease car for 30 months that includes the idea affected, along with a $50,000 check. This will show that the world that "people just like you and me can be creative." Every week, Americans will be waiting for and watching the latest Yankee Ingenuity TV advertisement promoting America's latest Idea Person. Ford and General Motors TV advertisements could become a cult culture TV special, just like American Idol. It's about time that Ford and General Motors executives understand that customers only buy cars from people they trust.

Many people will have a small suggestions, but once the mind is opened to being creative, no one knows who will turn up with the next big maximum award suggestion. Even in major league baseball not everyone can hit a home run every time, but by continually swinging away, the batting average goes up. The same positive encouragement on creativity will also work for the Yankee Ingenuity Suggestions Program. Yankee Ingenuity will become the "Idea Lottery" for those creative people who like to play the lottery.

Suggestions submitted through a dealership that have no material value can be awarded a service voucher for a free oil change at a local dealer. This way, local dealer traffic is increased, bringing potential customers into the dealer showroom at a much lower cost than those Sunday newspaper ads.

YANKEE INGENUITY NEWSLETTER

The Yankee Ingenuity Suggestion Program needs to have its own organ as part of the suggestion program. The newspaper will have three basic functions:

1. Personal recognition

2. Updates on how the suggestion program is doing

3. A method of communicating TRUST and INTEGRITY to the organization and customers, like the old *Ford Times* and the *Corvette News*. In the 1960s, you received *Corvette News* if you purchased a Corvette; why not do a *Yankee Ingenuity Suggestion Magazine* for every one that turns in a suggestion?

The Yankee Ingenuity Suggestion Newspaper has to include photos and stories about the person and their creative endeavor. Newspapers will be published every two weeks. The creativity of each unit needs to systematically communicate each contributor's approved suggestion by using the internal newspaper. The newsletter will be an excellent way to keep in contact in a positive, cost-effective way with all future customers. In this day and age, it may become an e-mail newsletter—very cost effective!

Also, Yankee Ingenuity Creativity Recognition Pages, with complete listings of the people and ideas, can be placed in the *Wall Street Journal* or *Time* magazine quarterlies.

CORPORATE RECOGNITION & SUPPORT

> Morale is faith in the man at the top.
> —Albert S. Johnstone

The highest-ranking corporate manager of each unit needs to walk around and personally recognize and thank each suggestion contributor from time to time. Personal recognition by supervision picks up employee spirits. This approach also makes management visible, improving the spiritual image and morale.

With the Message of Trust and Integrity, Sales Will Follow

In 1992, a vice president of an Automotive Division said to 135 executives in a CPC Engineering Leadership Meeting, "Less than 50% of the car-buying public ever steps foot in a General Motors dealership." Nineteen years later, that number has to be much lower because both Ford and General Motors are lucky to have 45% of the North American car and light truck market today.

The Yankee Ingenuity Suggestion Program will help get future customers identifying with the new corporate vision. The goal is to capture the American public's imagination and get the customer to step foot in showrooms. It's a form of innovative marketing. Suggestions that arrive by e-mail can now generate a creative Yankee Ingenuity customer list that can be used only for soft marketing of TRUST, HONESTY, and INTEGRITY as a way to bring lost customers back into the fold.

CORPORATE CREATIVITY WEBSITE

The Yankee Ingenuity Suggestion Program will become the pivotal base for a creativity website so everyone in cyberspace can work to help Ford and General Motors build better vehicles.

Corporate Creativity Website for Schoolchildren

Open up a creativity web site for schoolchildren of all ages. The goal will be to provide weekly creativity projects for each grade level three through twelve. There could be a soft message of seeking suggestions on how to improve the environment around us. Also, what would a child like to see in a car? The rewards could be intangible, with a Yankee Ingenuity Button or some cash for the next mall visit. **In just a few years these young people will be the next customers. They should be treated well.**

THE GOLD MINE

The Yankee Ingenuity Suggestion Program is a gold mine sitting right in Ford and General Motors' back yard. And, when properly functioning, it costs the corporations absolutely nothing, while providing billions of dollars in savings every year in return. That is billions of dollars in cash that Ford or General Motors did not have before the program started.

To get a program of this magnitude going requires a total commitment of initial funding and time by corporate top brass on down. Otherwise, it will end up just like any other "Program of the Month" the organizations have tried in the past. (See page 51.)

THE LEASE-RECYCLE PROGRAM

Recycling—the next industrial revolution.
—William McDonough and Michael Braungart, Atlantic
Monthly, *October 1998*

What trends could shape the American auto industry over the next several years and how can Ford and GM best position themselves today to weather the most likely changes ahead?

WHAT IS THE PROBLEM

The emerging, middleclass economies of both China and India are starting to demand products that require an ever-greater amount of raw materials. Within ten years, China and India will be using 40-50% of the world's raw materials. In 2008, China alone was purchasing and using about 20–25% of the Earth's raw materials on an annual basis; this was the cause of a major rise of raw material prices around the world. The global recession that started at the end of 2008 put a damper on cost increases, but once the economy starts to pick-up, the raw material prices will also begin to rise. As the U.S. dollar drops in value, and it is dethroned as the Worlds Reserve Currency, the price of raw materials will continue to increase.

Due to the laws of economics and inflation, the cost of raw materials could more than double, or triple, or possibly even reach greater multiples in price over the next ten years and Ford and General Motors will be locked into a totally resource-short world if management doesn't take a look at the global raw material picture now. Because of the projected costs for future raw and finished materials, it is imperative that the Strategic Planning department look at a total picture that also includes materials and future shipping costs as well as "off shoring." If Ford and the General Motors don't try to understand what is happening and take corrective action now, there won't even be one of the last two, true American automotive manufacturing organizations left standing in the next ten years. I cannot say it enough times, **a Strategic Plan for the procurement of raw materials is mandatory for survival.**

In 2008, the Detroit Big Three had problems with their pre-established parts contracts. With both Ford with its spin-off partner Visteon, and GM with its spin-off partner Delphi, cost problems were mostly based on escalating raw material costs. The raw material costs had been rising because of that age-old economic law of Supply and Demand. There was nothing the Big Three could do about it. Ford and GM in their current situations, without establishing a Strategic Raw Materials Plan, will wither and go the way of the Packard, Studebaker, and the Hudson Motor Car companies.

WHY THE PROBLEM NEEDS TO BE SOLVED, AND WHAT ARE THE IMPLICATIONS

The law of supply and demand determines the purchase price of raw materials. The United States' high labor costs and tax structure, combined with much higher raw material costs, will make it almost impossible to compete with foreign competition. For Ford and GM, it will be very difficult to survive under these conditions.

CHINA IS JUST TOO BIG TO IGNORE

Within a single generation, China has raised itself from a nation in abject poverty to an economic powerhouse—and all because of manufacturing, not the service industry. Today, China not only has the largest, but the fastest growing economy in the world. No doubt, the American consumption of Chinese goods and products has helped fuel China's growth to this point, but don't be alarmed in five years if China has the largest economy in the world, and the United States is number two.

I believe one of China's goals is to acquire the raw materials required to fuel their economy and military requirements. Remember a strong economy also fuels a strong military system. I also feel that this is the main reason China is helping to build roads and bridges in Africa. Not to help the Africans, but to have an infrastructure in place in order to remove raw materials easily.

At the present time, the Chinese Government has kept the rate of the yuan under-valued against international currencies in an effort to maintain China's meteoric growth. What is happening now is just the initial stage: Chinese businessmen in the future could form a consortium and buy a lot of the major U. S. corporations at market value, and it wouldn't even dent their wallets. Chinese business men purchased the Saginaw Steering Division from GM's spinoff Delphi Corporation and named it Nexsteer. I'm sure that Chinese business men have a few more deals in the works. When that happens, what will become of the previously agreed-to retirement plans? Under the impending circumstances, the retired workers and U.S. citizens can only hope for the best.

Qian Qichen, retired Chinese Vice Premier, 2004, was quoted in the official **China Daily** newspaper, November, 2004, edition. He said, "The U.S. is dreaming if it thought, the 21st century was the American century."

Please do not ever forget that China is still a communistic nation run by military men.

FORD AND GM BECOME PAPER COMPANIES

Let's talk about leasing first. Since 2005, leasing has become big business to the automotive personal vehicle market and, as an example, comprises over 50% of all vehicle transactions in the Detroit area dealerships of Hoot McInerney (Lincoln, Mercury, Dodge, and Toyota) today.

Ford and GM need to STOP selling cars altogether, and START leasing in 2016. In 2011 leasing is becoming a trend where more and more products are being leased. For instance, cell phones and laptop computers are being leased in greater numbers based on lower monthly charge and convenience.

When Ford and General Motors are able to offer quality, maintenance-free, fuel efficient, appealing vehicles that can be recycled every ten years for a new model, the lessees will become long-term coveted customers for the manufacturers and the dealers. Ford and General Motors will have a continuous revenue stream from each leased vehicle for a ten-year period, and as leased vehicles will be insured 100% through the joint Ford and GM Insurance Company, dealer's main goal will be to keep the customer happy each time the vehicle is serviced. They will also receive a percentage of the monthly payments on each lease package they sell.

In reality Ford and General Motors will be in the paper business: they will manufacture vehicles to sell paper. The lease agreement includes, vehicle lease, insurance, and 100% service all packaged as a one-paper agreement. Paper is where the profit's at, ask any banker. The goal will be to have all vehicles 100% leased by 2020.

VALUE LEADERS

In the first 70 years of the last century, General Motors made its mark by becoming America's automotive "Value Leader" in the industry. The Ford Motor Company firmly held on to second place, with the Chrysler Corporation solidly in third. If Ford and GM are to survive in the 21st century, they will have to become the value leaders with their respective vehicle offerings. Lexus, Toyota, and Honda have, for the most part, become America's value leaders today.

RECYCLING

Recycling vehicles will be vital for Ford and General Motors future. In fact, it could result in the improvement of both Ford and GM's economic growth. Also, recycling will help with the reduction of landfills and the reduction of emissions into the environment.

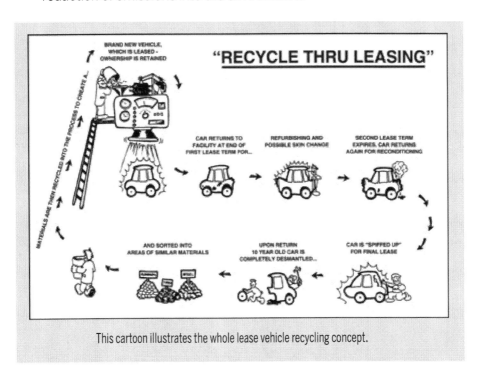

This cartoon illustrates the whole lease vehicle recycling concept.

A leased vehicle remains the property of the manufacturer, and in the case of Ford and General Motors, their products effectively store future raw materials as rolling stock.

Controlling and recycling the future raw material base will provide American jobs in the auto industry and preserve a much lower material cost base. When material costs are under control, the America automobile industry will be able to compete on a total product cost basis well into the next century. Without having full control of a low cost materials base, it will be very difficult for the last, two American automobile companies to compete with foreign vehicle manufactures who have better control of over raw material costs. Actually, if Ford and General Motors were saddled with both high material and labor costs, they would have to shift all manufacturing offshore into lower cost labor markets. If that were the case, both Ford and GM would dissolve into just a distribution and sales organization.

Nearly 65% of the average vehicle is made up of valuable components. Iron, steel, copper, and aluminum are the most easily recycled metals. When proper plastics and composites materials are selected, they can also be recycled cost effectively.

Recycling will also reduce the emission load by over one half. For example, the recycling of one ton of steel will eliminate the need to mine, ship, and process 2,500 pounds of iron ore, 1,400 pounds of coal, and 120 pounds of limestone—all which are needed to just to get to one (1) ton of steel ready for the processing stage.

Global demand for steel continues to grow, and although there are large amounts of steel capacity existing, much of it is actively in use. Beside automotive, steel is used for major household appliances, packaging, and many other things, including construction of roads, railways, infrastructure, and buildings and in a variety of other construction-related applications such as bolts, nails, and screws. Most large modern structures are supported by a steel skeleton. Other common applications include ship building, pipeline transport, mining, aerospace, heavy equipment, office equipment, steel wool, and vehicle armor.

Soaring steel demand has led to a big increase in the need for iron ore. China, which is undergoing a construction boom driven by its soaring economic growth, is the greatest consumer. China is even taxing the supply of iron ore coming from leading producers in Brazil and Australia. China also purchases scrap metals from U.S. material salvage companies. When vehicles (cars and trucks) are recycled today, the recycled materials are sold by scrap dealers at the going market price at the time of the sale. On April 26, 2011, the CEO of Ford, Allen Mulally stated, "Ford will be raising prices because of escalating commodity prices world-wide."

Right now, not every part of a car can be recycled, only 76% (by weight) is salvageable. Engineers have to reach a design goal of 95% reuse of automobile material to make the process inexpensive and accessible. This has to be done by both the Ford and General Motors organizations jointly to be truly cost effective. The Ford and General Motors Recycling Division will pool the resources from their car companies to work together in a united fashion in order to face the global competition head-on. I estimate that this program could collectively save Ford and GM about $30 billion a year. Engineers also need to make sure there is at least a 50% or more reduction of carbon dioxide emissions in the recycling process, over using base raw materials.

Recycling all salvageable materials at a fraction of their original costs will be one of the ways American automobile companies can compete on a global total cost basis. From the formation of Ford Motor Company in 1903, and General Motors in 1908, these last, two American automotive companies have always been working within a global economy, almost from day one. But now Ford and GM must deal with a new global economy that is changing the price of raw materials at a rapid speed because of the meteoric growth of both China and India. Because Ford and GM own the original material, they will achieve a lower material cost for their lease vehicles through recycling, and this will become lower still when balanced against overseas shipping costs, even with our higher U.S. labor rate costs.

Ford and GM should start a recycling program for leased vehicles in 2012, as an introduction to their total lease-recycle program of 2020.

The concept of lease-recycling was talked about by various GM advanced engineering and strategic planning people like Jim Paisley in the late 1970s, after the second oil embargo. At that time, I gave a lease-recycling presentation to the executive staff of a GM Division. In the presentation, I said, "By leasing a vehicle for ten years through various lessees, the company was effectively storing its future raw materials on the highway as rolling stock. The company will provide the lease policy, the insurance policy, and the service policy as one paper package. At this point the company will be building vehicles as a way to sell paper. GM will be in the paper business." They all looked so bewildered, I ended my presentation with:

THERE ARE FOUR TYPES OF PEOPLE IN THIS WORLD:
- PEOPLE THAT MAKE THINGS HAPPEN
- PEOPLE THAT WATCH THINGS HAPPEN
- PEOPLE WHO WONDER WHAT HAPPENED
- PEOPLE WHO DON'T CARE WHAT HAPPENS

After that presentation I'm sure they felt I was on drugs because the idea was so way over the top. They were unable to grasp the paper business concept.

PUTTING RECYCLING INTO PERSPECTIVE

Everyone on planet Earth is now living in a resource-short world. Every element in the Periodic Table needed to sustain a pleasant life is becoming in short supply, even down the elements in those eight glasses of water (H_2O) we need each day to keep our bodies properly flushed.

The situation will be greatly affected by a growing middle-class society in emerging nations around the world. When China and India step up man-

In 2010, India's Tata Motors introduced the Tata Nano, the world's most cost-effective vehicle (in the $2,500.00 range). The Tata Nano, could become the world's next new "Model T."

ufacturing to produce products and automobiles for domestic and export consumption, they could be using as much as 50% of the world's resources in raw materials and fossil fuels.

In 2010, the growing Chinese middle-class purchased over 15 million of the 54 million vehicles sold worldwide. That means that China now consumes over 27% of the world's auto production. Again, the message is that all of these new possessions require raw materials and energy to manufacture and operate, straining the world's raw material resources. India's middle-class will soon be the same size as the entire U.S. population.

Moreover, in the next 20 years, with India's growing economy, over 300,000,000 people could become the major part of India's new middle-class. Soon these people will also be bustling about in vehicles.

India and China's growing economies are in the process of absorbing 25–35 million new workers each year. Both countries will be shaping the 21st century global economy in their own image. Look for automobile manufacturing as the major staple to propel their economies forward.

China's goal to export automobiles to the United States rises from belief that the U.S. auto market is a bottomless pit of consumption. China only has to look to Japan and South Korea as exemplary models of solid economic growth with automobile production. Both Japan and Korea have kept their people working and their economy improving at the expense of the American worker. In reality, both Japan and Korea have transferred their unemployment to the American workforce.

When put into a global perspective, both Ford and General Motors are now living in a global economy where raw materials will become in very short supply.

AN ENTREPRENEUR TRIES TO DEVELOP A LEASE/RECYCLE VEHICLE
A good idea never dies, but it can lie dormant until the time is right. In 1994, an enterprising business-man, John T. Leavitt, tried to introduce a total recyclable/lease vehicle called the ETHOS that had a revolutionary low profile horizontal four-cylinder opposed, eight-piston (end to end) engine, with two counter-rotating crankshafts for balance. The goal was to introduce the vehicle through a K-Mart or Walmart network of stores, with the vehicles capable of being serviced through the store's automotive service departments while the customer shopped. It was very difficult to secure funding. The John Leavitt ETHOS vehicle was as revolutionary in 1994 as the Preston Tucker TUCKER vehicle back in 1948. Again it appears the timing was not right.

RECYCLE THROUGH LEASING: A LONG-TERM STRATEGIC PLAN

The Ford and GM Recycling Division should market their new, automotive Zero Waste Program in the following ways:

- Ford and GM should be the sole sponsor and derive all of the benefits

- Vehicle design will use the quality standard of 24 Sigma. The Honeywell Corporation's Home Products Division has been using the 24 Sigma Quality Standard since 1984. Their parts are so perfect, they have to only check 5 parts in a million. They have virtually no warranty program. It's a tremendous cost savings by doing it right the first time. Quality is very profitable when there are zero warranty costs.

- Vehicles will be designed and engineered for a 12-year product life. Actual vehicle product life is only 10 years; the overkill design feature will assure total customer satisfaction of quality, dependability, and vehicle performance. Always remember, when dealing with products, **"Quality is remembered long after price is forgotten."**

- Design each vehicle to stand out in its own product niche, wearing only one corporate badge. Put all the effort into making each brand a stand-out, not four or five re-badged, indistinguishable, and mediocre clones.

- Each lease package is designed for a 30-month lease. The vehicle will be leased four times in its product life.

- Design the vehicle to be reconditioned every 30 months. Three refurbishing conditioning processes over the ten-year vehicle product life, one after the first 30 months, and the second after the next 30 months (at the end of each 30 month lease period the vehicle will also receive a minor face lift). The ability to offer refurbished and updated vehicles to second, third, and forth lessees will offer an excellent challenge for corporate designers and engineers. It's the challenges that make designing and engineering vehicles fun; they will jump at the chance.

- Design and engineer vehicles for an 180,000-mile full-vehicle, bumper-to-bumper warranty as part of the lease package, because Ford and GM own the vehicle. The standard base mileage calculation will start at 15,000 miles per year for a total 150,000-mile product life.

- Design and engineer vehicles for a CAFE average of 50+ MPG. Most of the initial plug-in hybrid vehicles should be powered by CNG.

- Design vehicles to have a 50% less carbon dioxide footprint over predecessor vehicles they are replacing. This shows the consumer that Ford and GM are acting in harmony with the environment.

- Design all lease vehicles to be recycled 100% by the Ford and General Motors Recycling Division.

- Ford and General Motors will own all materials. The materials will have been being paid for at the program inception. The costs of raw materials will more than double or triple in a ten-year time frame. Yet the recycled material costs to Ford and GM should be less than 20% of the initial cost. Ford and GM will be able to compete on cost basis with anyone in the world, and will again become the world's value leaders.

- Lease rates will be reduced for each year the vehicle is in service.

- There will be no haggling over price; everyone will be offered the same fair and honest market value based on vehicle age in months, mileage, condition, and all the written and established variables.

- The lease plan will provide sharp-looking vehicles that will have complete worry-free service for their entire life.

- Properly managed by each marketing division of Ford or General Motors, there will be a lease vehicle to fit every pocketbook. Taking a page from GM's Alfred P. Sloan's marketing philosophy, "A car for every purse and purpose."

- When the consumer understands they are being provided real value at a fair price, everyone will be happy. In the future everyone will now trust a car salesperson. That will be a revelation in itself.

- As a special perk value to customers, lease exchanges could include an exchange for a pick-up truck or van when needed for a two- to four-week period. Lease rates will be adjusted to the value of the exchange vehicle.

- The goal will be to make leasing a recyclable vehicle from Ford or GM a totally rewarding experience, and also help Mother Earth in the process. (See more about this below.)

- All vehicles will be equipped with a black box data recorder to determine and validate all vehicle abuse for price adjustment.

- Lease vehicles will become a more uniform production volume schedule, and will enable Ford and General Motors to run their joint manufacturing plants 24/7/365 days a year, with a four-shift operation for maximum efficiency—one more shift then Henry Ford used in 1913 with his $5 per day wage. Now that's productivity with full utilization of all plant facilities and people.

- Run production plants based on vehicle actuarial data. Vehicle product lifespan can be tracked on an actuarial basis to provide vehicle recycle scheduling by monitoring all service work required. When customers purchase a car these days, the dealer has no idea when the customer would like a new car. With a lease vehicle, the dealer knows exactly when the customer will need a new car.

FORD AND GENERAL MOTORS GO GREEN

Not only is recycling through leasing the prudent thing to do as a way to provide low cost materials in the future, but recycling is also vital to improving the corporate image. Ford and General Motors will be seen as caretakers of the planet. The Greenies will all love Ford and GM for finally becoming honestly and truthfully green, not only by words but also by deeds.

> If you want one year of prosperity, plant corn. If you want ten years of prosperity, plant trees. If you want one hundred years of prosperity, educate people. —Chinese proverb

This image will allow them to provide a series of "conservation of materials" presentations to schoolchildren. Both Ford and General Motors jointly will visit schools (6th grade through 12th grade) across America to explain the Recycle Program. The Lease/Recycle Program will be reinforced with television advertisement, and tied into the Yankee Ingenuity Suggestion program. (See page 148.)

Success is not a matter of desire, but the product of a lot of hard work.
—**Jack Barringer**

The American auto industry needs to prove they have the vision, the leadership, and the technology to manufacture high mileage vehicles that reduce greenhouse gases. It's about time Ford and General Motors take a visionary leadership role and show the entire world what can be done through recycling and Yankee Ingenuity.

PART FIVE: MANAGEMENT

MARKETING AND ADVERTISING

HUMAN RESOURCES

SPIRITUAL LEADERSHIP FOR THE AUTO INDUSTRY

MARKETING AND ADVERTISING

Jim Dollinger's *Four Pillars for Market Share and the Twenty Steps for Greatness* still have value for both Ford and General Motors today. I have found that automotive manufacturing operations can produce a large number of vehicles, but the real job is selling them. In this post-millennium world, it will take the application of Jim Dollinger's sales and marketing skills to enhance the last, two American automobile companies' sales figures.

FIRST, A BIT ABOUT JAMES MICHAEL DOLLINGER

James M. Dollinger (a.k.a. Buickman) has sold over 25,000 new and used GM vehicles so far in his career, and is known as being one of the top automotive salesmen in the U.S. Recognized as GM's top Buick salesman, he has received the prestigious "Billy Durant Award" for his sales excellence. Jim has 35 years in selling GM vehicles.

Some time ago, Jim pointed out to me that the people in charge of sales and marketing at General Motors have little to no actual retail sales experience. A three-month internship at a dealership does not provide the knowledge and experience to run a large auto company's sales and marketing program. When the people in charge have very little understanding of what it takes to run a dealership, errors and marketing blunders are made at every corner. In 2004, Jim founded the website: www.General-Watch.com to provide complete reporting on GM. Guess what, General Motors wanted to close down Jim's website.

Jim Dollinger's writings do not cover product offerings relative to style or engineering content. Dealers make comments to the corporation from time to time as to customer preference of options, styling, and color and Strategic Planning has an understanding of what competitor vehicle companies are offering, so Jim has focused his efforts on
marketing and selling vehicles at the dealership level. Jim's writing, although addressed to General Motors, will also have similar application at Ford.

James M. Dollinger has been nominated to the General Motors Board of Directors, but failed to secure enough votes to obtain a board seat. Jim is a person who makes things happen, and he finds it frustrating when he has to deal with people who don't care what happens. In 2005, Jim was also raising the flag that GM was headed toward bankruptcy. Of course, that occurred in June 2009.

THE PLAN: A RETURN TO GREATNESS

By Jim Dollinger

FOUR PILLARS:

1st PILLAR: CUSTOMER LONG-TERM CARE

2nd PILLAR: DEALER TRAINING

3rd PILLAR: COMPANY POLICY

4th PILLAR: VETERAN INVOLVEMENT

Introduction

This outline contains the first 20 ideas for improvement. Many more exist, however, these 20 illustrate the existence of rational, executable ideas. GM management complains of healthcare costs, retirement expenses and exchange rates while continuing their empty promises of new products, processes and restructuring. We all are aware of the repeated failures in the marketplace.

These past decades of decline are attributable to GM's failures in merchandising rather than costs; costs which in truth are incidental to the real problem. Sales executives at General Motors don't understand marketing. They don't know how to sell cars. It's all about image and perception. A winning image in the marketplace can overcome product weakness, assuming the product is not glaringly inferior. Given today's relative equality of merchandise, my experience is that the presentation makes the difference.

Since 1997, after watching the missteps of GM management, I began developing a marketing plan specifically for General Motors. It uses proven techniques learned through decades of successful selling and sales management. In addition to retailing well in excess of ten thousand new vehicles, I have also studied the corporation's historical development. I've attended annual meetings since 1982 and hosted luncheon PowerPoint presentations on market share. As the nation's leading Buick salesman six times, and the General Manager of 6 different GM stores, my success has been significant.

This year, for the fifth year in a row, I have been nominated for the Board of Directors. In support of that nomination, I offer a few of the ideas from **The Plan: A Return to Greatness**.

Any plan is only as good as its implementation. Having a successful out-line is one thing, but if it is not put into effect in a logical sequence, the odds of success greatly diminish.

Alfred Sloan, the architect of the modern GM, years ago instituted an idea called the Ten Day Report. The implementation of The Plan builds upon this idea. Once A Return to Greatness is announced, GM should release the Step One. Subsequently, we issue another improvement in ten days, continuing a pattern of one step every ten days. This will create anticipation and the image of leadership. The groups targeted for action will look forward to the next event, and come to understand that there is a purpose and direction emanating from the company. I hope each of you will visit www.GeneralWatch.com where background information can be found. A copy of the PowerPoint presentation detailing strategy and structure is also available for download.

A RETURN to GREATNESS

The Improvements

STEP ONE: Elimination of Destination Charges

The Return announcement proclaims: If you want to pay freight, get a foreign car. This is mindful of Iacocca's proclamation, "If you can find a better deal, take it." This worked for Lee, and showed his tenacity. He earned Chrysler respect and admiration by showing true lead-ership. He had gumption and people like that. It's an attraction. The problem with GM is that we are seen as softies—and losers. Taking a stance, and actually giving customers something easy to understand and appreci-ate, will be a tremendous opening salvo. It will set the competition back on their heels and let people know we are serious. This step begins our weaning process from the devastation of rebates. We can work towards effective net pricing and earn goodwill in the process.

STEP TWO: Elimination of Mid-Year Price Increases

Ten days after the original announcement, we release the next step. The deceptive practice of incremental increases only clouds the purchase process. Customers will perceive us as doing something positive and beneficial, rather than sneaky and underhanded. We will earn more goodwill without any true expense.

STEP THREE: Quarterly Incentive Changes.

No more pressure to Buy now, hurry before it ends, only to be followed by another program. This repetitious process, which has been our norm, destroys credibility and works against us in many ways. How many times has a customer purchased, only to have the rebate increase the very next day? The effect of this goofiness has customers riding around in their new cars, upset that they just missed an opportunity.

Let's create some stability, and simplicity, in the marketplace. Give customer's confidence in their decisions, and provide the right amount of time to make informed choices. Give the customer the opportunity of ordering the vehicle of their liking, without worrying what the deal might be. Also, allow the retail personnel an appropriate amount of time to properly sell and deliver the unit. This would be preferable to slam-dunking folks who are under the gun to meet a deadline, and who end up less than completely satisfied with their delivery process. Quarterly adjustments only make sense and give the business a well-needed sense of order.

STEP FOUR: Destination Detroit

This idea brings all future, award-winning dealers and salespeople to the Motor City. The benefits are countless. First, we would be more effective in focusing the meetings and events on the business at hand. Rather than desert tours and polo matches, we entertain showing Motown's finest offerings.

Have the individuals tour Milford Proving Grounds, drive on the test track and witness a crash in order to illustrate safety testing. They can go through the Styling Studio and expose future designs. Allow them to meet with engineers and see the inner workings of corporate headquarters. Also, pamper the spouses with our city's best services.

At the conclusion, send them back home ecstatic about GM—and Detroit. These actions would build goodwill for our city and company throughout the country. Meanwhile, our executives can stay at home, which would be very good for their family lives and our expense column.

STEP FIVE: Home Deliveries

We announce an effort of working with our dealers to bring to the customer the vehicle of their choice, directly to their place of employment or residence. Most customers dread, even dislike, the dealer experience. Offering this free service would further build goodwill and lead to customer appreciation.

I've made an entire career out of this offering. People absolutely love it and this Step alone is responsible for more sales than anything I've ever done. Once we begin this process, our competition will probably follow—but hey, we'll be seen as the leader for a change.

STEP SIX: Got GM—Get GM

It is a loyalty incentive anyone can comprehend. If you currently own or lease a GM vehicle, you receive $1,000. It is stackable and compatible with any offering. It's also transferable to family member residing at the same address. No goofy rebate if you own a non-GM car. Who thought of that one anyway? Why reward disloyalty, or have to ask customers if they own a competitive product? Let's only give something to those who already support us. If the customer is not eligible, oh well: next time they will be. The program should be renewed annually and left in force all year.

STEP SEVEN: Annual Model Change

This is big. Sloan came up with this idea for a reason—it evened out the seasonal fluctuations in sales. Whoever got the bright idea to come out with a car whenever it's ready really did not understand the car business. How many of you remember the anticipation of the fall's New Model Introductions? Let's return to the regular release of new products after Labor Day, and return a sense of order to the business.

These days we're selling three different model years side by side. That is very confusing and damaging. Some things should never change, and this is one of those things.

STEP EIGHT: Dealer Margin

We will let our retail partners know they have something to gain in our quest to regain share. For each full point of share we regain, we give the dealers another point of margin. They can use this additional margin to do more advertising or award salesperson incentives. They could increase levels of service, carry more inventory, hire additional staff or retain extra profit. The dealers are the ones with the investment, and they best understand their local markets. Let them decide what to do with the money. Maybe multi-line dealers will see the benefit in moving our products, rather than those of the competition.

STEP NINE: Day at the Dealer

Each month, every salaried member of the Vehicle, Sales, Service and Marketing (VSSM) would be required to spend one day in a randomly selected dealership service department, preferably in write-up. This activity would build tremendous goodwill, and give our employees valuable insight into the customer's needs and wants. Actually getting to know GM employees would give customers a sense that GM has a face. They would begin to see GM as human beings, rather than an impersonal Corporation. The dealers would benefit by having additional support in their service lanes, thereby offering quicker, more responsive service on those days when executives were there to assist. Customer satisfaction would increase, as would repeat and referral business.

STEP TEN: AARP

This is a fantastic demographic, and yet another opportunity to simplify incentives. Make it a year-round program. If you belong to AARP, you get $500 off any GM product, buy or lease. Make it compatible with all other offerings, then leave it alone. People ask about it all the time anyway. They feel cheated seeing it after they've already made a deal.

STEP ELEVEN: Brand Merchandise

Include with each delivery a coupon for $50 off, or to-wards, merchandise from an affinity catalog. For each brand, have a booklet full of things such as shirts, sweaters, gym bags, coats, golf bags, etc. The end result would be people going to nightclubs and health clubs, churches and stores, sporting our logos, and providing us with free advertising. This activity is of a personal nature, and would do wonders toward building strong brand image and awareness.

STEP TWELVE: Auto Shows

Instead of the current practice of giving rebates to certain residents of surrounding counties, let's offer Auto Show tickets to those who test-drive our products. This would bring people into the stores and provide an inexpensive gift that would be remembered as the customers enter and exit the shows. We would be the good guys who gave them something concrete as the sponsor of their attendance. The gift could possibly be made to include early entrance or special access on certain days.

STEP THIRTEEN: Profit Sharing

At year-end, instead of giving our employees a cash award for profit sharing, give them the choice of common stock. Have them become true partners in the company's success. Owning stock would increase employee perception that they are part of something, and would be more meaningful in the long term than a few dollars easily disposed of.

STEP FOURTEEN: Executive Cars

Quite often, GM executives turn in their factory demos with the odometer just under the next price discount level. This practice is both frustrating and annoying. The inconsiderate action toward fellow employees and retirees is inexcusable and unacceptable. GM needs to announce a policy of driving the unit to the next mileage category whenever the driver is within say 250 miles of the next price break. How can the company promote unity when a few individuals think they are being cute? I've seen units turned in three miles short of the next discount more than once. What does this do for morale?

STEP FIFTEEN: Referral Savings Account

Similar to the GM Card (another crisis), GM announces a program to accumulate savings of $50 for each referral who buys or leases a new vehicle. The referral must be disclosed prior to delivery, and would be similar to what we commonly refer to as a birddog." The account holder could then cash the savings in at the time they take delivery of their own unit.

STEP SIXTEEN: Free GM Smart Care Maintenance Agreement to all GM Retirees

This 36-month / 36,000 mile program would offer free, recommended maintenance to all GM retirees. The benefit would be great for bringing customers in for dealer service. This group of people has tremendous purchasing power and exerts a large amount of influence over their family members' buying decisions, often contributing financially to the transaction. Also, increased showroom traffic by our service customers would lead to increased sales to those individuals and to others who feel more comfortable buying when there is heightened activity.

STEP SEVENTEEN: GM Card

This was one of the best programs GM ever had. That was, until someone decided to take earnings away from eligible GM family members and thereby alienate thousands of employee cardholders. Many people swore off GM for the move. Some form of retribution needs to be made. Consultations with the legal staff could result in some form of program to attempt to bring those lost back into the fold.

STEP EIGHTEEN: Sales Guilds

For years GM had brand-specific sales guilds. Now, everything is combined into the GM Mark of Excellence. It's a decent enough program, but there would be a greater impact if we returned to the old days of Buick Salesmaster, and the Chevrolet Legion of Leaders. These former groups built a sense of loyalty and awareness for each carline, and gave salespeople their own individual rankings within respectively common professions.

STEP NINETEEN: Direct Factory Communication

So, you go to your local dealer and order a new vehicle. After that, silence. You might receive a call from your salesman with an update as to the order status, but usually, no contact is made until the vehicle arrives. Utilizing the Internet, GM could send information directly to the customer, informing them of their order's progress at the various stages, including when the vehicle is scheduled for production, after it is actually built (including the new VIN), and the estimated shipping and arrival dates. This increased communication would lead to greater awareness and satisfaction, as well as anticipation.

STEP TWENTY: Reinstatement of GM Regional Sales Training Classes

Years ago, GM offered professional sales development classes at the Regional Training Centers. As one who attended these seminars, I can attest to the benefit of the experience. I learned many things that still contribute to my success, even to this very day. Who better than GM to train salespeople as to the proper way to present our products, and follow up with our customers? The manufacturer knows more about the product than anyone and should be able to give competitive information beneficial to those who need it in today's hotly contested environment. I believe this is far superior to our current system of computer testing and merit award requirements. I'd say roughly half of the time, savvy salespeople subcontract their computer testing to those more adept at answering multiple choice and working online. This process sidesteps the purpose of giving our salespeople the information in the first place, not to mention improving their competitive performance.

These twenty illustrations from The Plan are an indication of the kinds of marketing that will lead to a rebound in GM's sales. As you can see, there would be hardly any expense involved, and in fact, many of the ideas would actually serve to reduce costs. GM needs to get off of the fire sale, deal-of-the-day mentality. The full-page, distress ads currently running only harm image and create a sense of desperation. GM needs to let it go and save the dough. We spend tens of millions of dollars unnecessarily, including huge amounts for useless spokesmen who bring nothing to the table.

Additional steps in The Plan include things like further doing away with rebates. If there is a problem with day's supply, don't increase the rebate. Instead, add a point or two to the residual value and have the image of a good car with a great lease, as opposed to a slow mover with a big rebate.

GM needs to wake up and realize, as the book says, "Your Marketing Sucks." GM worries about healthcare costs and pension benefits yet wastes untold millions in the name of marketing. To quote my friend Jerry Flint, senior automotive writer at Forbes magazine, "It's not that the leaders of GM are bad people, they're not. They just don't understand the American car business." He further states, "This business really isn't all that difficult, all it takes is a good car and someone to sell it." Jerry Flint passed away August 7, 2010 from a stroke.

This excerpt from *The Plan: A Return to Greatness* shows that this someone does exist. Articles about my achievements and ideas have been showcased in major publications such as The Detroit News and Automotive News. However, there is nothing better than a first-hand look at specific examples and detailed explanations.

General Watch News
Market Capitalization

May 2000	... $66 Billion
May 2001	... $48 Billion
May 2004	... $25 Billion
May 2005	... $15 Billion
May 2006	... $12 Billion
May 2007	... $19 Billion
May 2008	... $5 Billion
May 2009	... Bankrupt

Under the leadership of G. Richard Wagoner (Executive Vice President and President North American Operations 1994, President and Chief Operating Officer 1998, Chief Executive Officer 2000, and Chairman 2003) General Motors has closed, sold, or spun off:

Oldsmobile
Hughes
Daewoo
Delphi
Detroit Diesel
Defense Electronics
Light Armored Vehicles
American Axle
Electromotive
EDS and more!
GM Desert Proving Grounds
Isuzu
Pontiac
Saturn
Hummer
Saab
Medium Duty Trucks
Fiat Fiasco - Payment

HUMAN RESOURCES

For the past 25 years, the Detroit Big Three have been continually search-ing for a structural solution to the spiritual problem, and it hasn't worked. Only when the American auto industry understands that it has not been a structural problem but a spiritual problem that has hampered their return to profitability, will they return to profits.

The spiritual problem concerns understanding that people are a com-pany's greatest asset. Only by learning how to use the creative strengths of each and every employee wisely will the Detroit Big Three ever return to profitability.

WORK ENVIRONMENT

The work environment has changed in the past 25 years, and so have profits. Gone from all three corporations are the annual summer picnics, where the division or smaller operating units would rent an amusement park for a total family/company outing. It was these company-spon-sored get-togethers that helped tie the work unit into a more productive and cohesive force, a force where everyone felt part of the company fam-ily. The goal was, *A happier workforce, a more productive workforce.* The picnics and open-house functions made employees proud of where they worked and offered a chance to show their family what they did, along with providing a sense of belonging.

Today's executives and bean-counters view those functions as a total waste of money. No one cares anymore about workforce unity. Employee value has been totally taken out of the profit equation and all decisions are focused on the bottom-line, which continues to run a brighter red each year.

RETIREMENT

In the gentler times of the 1960s, 70s, and 80s, most employees retired at age 65. When the UAW hourly workers on the line retired, it was usually one last trip to the beer garden with friends as a retirement send-off. But when any of the Detroit Big Three salaried employees retired, it was a bigger deal and honored the employee's contribution to the company. The higher the salaried employee was in the food chain, the more extreme the party. In some cases the retiree's spouse and children were also invited to hear unique work stories of the retiree's life. Some of the retirement parties for the higher-ups at the Cadillac Motor Division in the 1960s would go on for hours after the official recognition and celebration, by playing cards, drinking, and shooting craps.

As the auto industries MBA financial people started to gain control of the operational function of the corporation in the early 1980s, the whole demeanor of employee retirement parties changed. The MBA (Masters of Business Administration) degree was the key to success, and almost a requirement in order to be promoted within the higher ranks of management. What it meant though, was that American auto company decisions were no longer made from the heart. All decisions were only based on the short-term bottom-line. Many retirees to this day feel that it was the corporate MBAs that sucked the life out of all three companies—Ford, GM, and Chrysler.

In the past, many Detroit Big Three retirees enjoyed their work and the people they worked for because it gave them a sense of value, and they worked very hard to earn it. For some, the last day at work was most difficult: walking out for the last time after years of dedication. For others, it meant giving up the friendly working environment, their friends, and their identity. It seems many people retiring in the 50s, 60s, 70s, and 80s all identified themselves through their work, and find their work and the work social environment to be an integral part of the fabric of their life. When employees retire after years of service to a company, they would like to retire on their terms, not terms dictated by the company.

> The harder you work, the harder it is to surrender.
> —Vince Lombardi

Many retirees experienced difficulty retiring early, as all of the Detroit Big Three offered early retirement packages or buy-outs. Those who decided to take the early retirement found the change was difficult, and some are still adjusting. Some retirees that took the early retirement packages, or were forced into early retirement, had depression problems. Others required medical depressants to cope with their sudden change in life. On the other side of the coin, a few retirees were happy to take the early out and escape the drudgery because all of the fun had gone out of their job, and going to work.

Health Benefit Cutbacks

One of the major concerns of retirement is the fear of running out of money. The shift of healthcare costs onto retiree shoulders has added an additional burden to their financial concerns.

On July 15, 2008, CEO Rick Wagoner announced that GM salaried retirees would no longer receive healthcare coverage. The announcement sent GM retirees into a state of shock. (Fortunately, the former factory workers have a union contract that prevents the company from revoking their coverage.) Some white collar workers said, "If I knew we were going to be treated this poorly, I would have joined a union." The Big Three gave salary personnel all the benefits that were given to the union workers so salary people would not form a union.

> Crisis are nature's way
> of forcing change.
> —Susan Taylor

To help white-collar retirees pay for their new healthcare burden, GM then announced that they were raising monthly pension payments by $300, typically meaning an additional $240 to $255 after taxes. That sum comes from the same funds as the GM monthly retirement check, not, as in the past, out of GM's current operating budget. This manipulation added billions of dollars to GM's bottom-line, yet they still had to file for bankruptcy.

The Detroit Big Three employees were promised healthcare, vision, and dental benefits in their retirement years—promises that now appear far greater than the auto industry can afford! But promises are promises, and Ford (who cut benefits in 2007) and GM went back on those promises. Many retirees feel they were lied to, and no longer trust the management teams. Some retirees are down right pissed-off as they see the reduction of healthcare benefits as a way for the Ford and GM Executive Management Teams to save their sorry asses.

Retirement Benefits

A GM retiree with a very large family—lots of children and grandchildren—all of driving age and some in businesses that used light trucks, told this story recently at a GM group luncheon. The retiree's family had used his discount to buy several vehicles every year. After about ten years, he received a letter from GM stating that his discount was being canceled (for a year or so) because he was using it outside the rules of the agreement. He was asked to prove that the purchases over the years were made by members of his family in order to maintain his discount. The retiree sent several letters, with questions, and got no response. His family—minus their discount—began to buy foreign makes. Over the last five years, his family has now purchased a number of Toyotas and Hondas. They like the quality and they are not going back to GM vehicles.

Retirees feel violated when they are treated like doormats after giving over 40-plus years of their life to a company. They do retaliate!

The Golden Retirement Card

During the 1980s and early-1990s, retirees were given a special Golden Retirement Identification Card. This allowed, even invited retirees to walk inside GM just like the old days to visit friends. The Golden Identification Card was a touch of class.

Today, if any of the Detroit Big Three retirees think they can use their Golden IDs to visit the old workplace, they are whistling Dixie.

In the first decade of the 21st century, all the class has gone out of the American auto industry. Retirees recognize that auto industry employees no longer live in a world where they are valued for skills, now it's just dollars and headcount. Employees are looked upon and valued as burdens. Sad but true! And the major goal is to reduce burdens at all costs.

THE HUMAN FACTOR

Just before Christmas, and at the end of his first year of retirement, a retiree I know got a letter from GM that his December retirement check would be reduced. An audit had shown that he had worked one year less than what was used to determine his monthly check; he'd been paid about $150 a month too much. That brought the total overpayment to about $2000, so, his just before Christmas his check was zip.

Okay, everyone agrees an error was made. However, the letter inferred that the error was the retiree's fault. Annoyed, the retiree called the appropriate GM office and suggested that this whole issue had been very poorly handled from a personnel point of view. The retiree suggested that GM should deduct the $2000 overpayment over the following year, in other words, over the same amount of time during which GM had made the error. The response was that this couldn't be done because, the retiree might die before GM got their money back!

This retiree did the only thing he could, he retaliated and has now purchased a Toyota Prius for himself and a RAV4 for his daughter. It's been over a year and he's not dead yet. He will probably purchase many more Toyotas in the future.

The list of bungled personnel issues goes on and on because no one is applying common sense to human problems. Everything corporate must relate to the bottom-line. No one listens to the mediating circumstances.

LOOKOUTAMERICA.ORG
The above comments come from retirees responding to my website, plus direct conversations with retirees when we get together each month for lunch. My website, Lookoutamerica.org, has provided an opportunity for automotive retirees to express their true feelings. They have no other place to go where someone will listen to them. The website has provided that forum, almost like the complaint department at a large department store after Christmas. Lookoutamerica.org has given retirees a space to vent their anger on how they feel they have been unfairly treated after many years of dedicated service.

Company Loyalty Is Fading

Retirees are now starting to use the same cost cutting rules as the Detroit Big Three. It's just like the line in "The Godfather," "Sorry, it's just business." In the Fort Myers, Florida area, a few Detroit Big Three retirees are bolting from their company's vehicle employee purchase plan as a way to save money and cover the costs of the reneged healthcare. The current, money-saving vehicle is the Kia. As one retiree stated, "It is now more cost effective to purchase a Kia with a better warranty than a Buick."

Many retirees feel that when the American auto industry finally wakes up and realizes that the retirees made up one of the largest and most loyal customer bases they had, it will be too late—they'll have blown it!

The gate with the word LOYALTY on it swings in both directions. As another of Detroit's favorite lines goes these days, "Don't let the loyalty gate hit you in the ass on the way out."

That said, when the U.S. auto industry starts building a plug-in/CNG hybrid that can be fueled at home, I will buy it in a New York minute.

When the buying public realizes that even the Detroit Big Three retirees are no longer purchasing their vehicles because they no longer trust the company, outside sales will also drop. The perception is that since the American auto industry reneged on benefits to retirees—and General Motors openly admitted to building poor quality products— the Detroit auto companies are not trustworthy. This being the case, might they renege on warranty issues in the future on a purchased vehicle? Look at some of the GM retiree stockholders who lost a lot of money when GM declared bankruptcy. If the retirees and former stockholders don't trust the company, why should the buying public?

When I started writing this book in 2006, my wife and I owned a Buick, a Cadillac, and a Toyota Camry Hybrid I later purchased in protest, because the Saturn Aura Single Mode Hybrid I had ordered was a total marketing sham.

This last year, we gave my wife's Buick (6 years old with only 42,000 miles) to her daughter, but not before doing extensive warranty work at our own expense. The wheel bearing failure did it for me, but my wife, Jan, was a loyal Buick owner and liked the 2011 Buick Regal. Unfortunately, the two colors she admired were not available for another six months. If the Buick dealer could have promised the delivery of a RED Regal in 2 months, we would of purchased the vehicle on the spot. Vehicle shopping would have been over; men hate to shop. Then she checked out the new Chevrolet Volt and was impressed by the technology. Sorry, again she would have to wait a year or more to get a chance to purchase the vehicle. Finally, as a retired GM employee's wife, she looked at and drove a Cadillac sedan with letters for a name, but was not that excited.

Some years back, I noticed my wife admiring a Lexus on the road and I said to her, "Someday I will buy you a Lexus." One thing I have learned later in life is, "Women Never Forget Anything You Tell Them, Especially a Promise." I am a man of my word.

And a "Promise is a Promise." When she drove the Lexus, she liked the quality, style, performance, and everything else about the vehicle. I'm 73, so we purchased her Lexus with a seven-year warranty package directly from the company so I will be almost 80 before I have to look for another vehicle for my wife. I try to do everything correctly, and my wife's red Lexus was delivered with a big red bow on the roof the day before Christmas.

Last year, we gave one daughter the Buick, and the other daughter got a down payment on a 2009 Chevrolet HHR, so we still have helped the GM cause. But as a retiree, I now look at my loyalty to GM the same way GM looks at its loyalty toward their retirees and GM stockholders, and that's the way life is. (I still have a printed GM Stock Certificate from the Old GM as a souvenir of a once-great company.)

Presently, we own a Cadillac, a Camry Hybrid, and a Lexus. I have no guilty conscious because I have a happy wife. Again, GM was not able to deliver the cars she was interested in, a red Buick Regal or a Chevrolet Volt. Both vehicles were not available for six months to a year. Why should the customer have to compromise or wait six months for a red Regal because GM does not have its act together?

IT'S REALLY THAT SIMPLE

Most people won't purchase a product or service from someone they don't trust.

In the sales and marketing community, as Tom Peters says, **"Perception is everything."** It comes down to trust, and many retirees no longer trust their former employers—Ford, General Motors, or Chrysler/Fiat. Like it or not, it all comes down to that old saying, "Screw me once, shame on you. Screw me twice, shame on me." Based on that principle, many former customers, retirees, and stockholders are long gone.

Salesmen who are trying to sell American auto industry vehicles are working long hours to provide for their families. They are also being caught in the middle on the trust issue.

RETIREES AND THE ANNUAL STOCKHOLDERS MEETING

At the 2007 General Motors Annual Stockholders Meeting in Wilmington, Delaware, GM Chairman and CEO Rick Wagoner faced much criticism from shareholders.

As a GM retiree, my wife and I (we represented over 2% of GM stockholders present) attended the 2007 Annual GM Stockholders Meeting along with 94 other shareholders.

We had the pleasure of sitting in the front row next to Ms. Evelyn Y. Davis.

Evelyn Davis, a feisty shareholder activist, known as the corporate gadfly, was the first to speak to Rick Wagoner. Her opening statement was: "Rick, you are a good-looking man, but being a good-looking man does not make you a good CEO. You are an asshole". Everyone was smiling as she spoke, including Rick Wagoner.

She then continued, asking Mr. Wagoner if GM could be a takeover target. He assured Evelyn Davis GM was not going private.

When it was my turn to speak, I recommended to GM Chairman Rick Wagoner that he put Lee Iacocca on GM's Board of Directors, or place him as an adviser to the Board of Directors. With Lee Iacocca on GM's Board of Directors, GM's stock would at least triple in value based on Lee's automotive experience, his ability to work with the UAW, and most of all, just his plain common sense. Bob Lutz, sitting next to Wagoner, thought the suggestion was outrageous and rolled his eyes. That was about the only time Bob Lutz was awake; he slept through most of the 2007 Annual Stockholders Meeting. Cameras and tape recorders were not permitted in the meeting—I guess GM did not want any photos or recordings of the charade taking place.

Lutz was later chastised during the meeting by another GM stockholder for his smug arrogance, disrespect, and total contempt for GM stockholders. The clapping of hands from the shareholders present made Lutz, Wagoner, and the GM Board of Directors get the message collectively. The majority of the less than 100 GM stockholders in the audience were retirees.

GM executives kept to a fully-structured 2 and a half-hour stockholder's meeting with the GM Board of Directors sitting up front like little crystal statues on display, dominated and under the full control of the GM Chairman. If Rick Wagoner didn't like what he was hearing, the stockholder was told to "Go sit down." So un-American!

This was in a stark contrast to Warren Buffet's 8 and a half-hour open forum stockholder's meeting with over 30,000 in attendance (2009). By the way, Warren Buffet and Charlie Munger of Berkshire Hathaway take unscripted questions from shareholders in the audience. There are no rules—shareholders may ask any question on their mind. Berkshire Hathaway does not end the stockholder's meeting until every stockholder is satisfied.

Comparing General Motors, who had lost billions and billions of dollars annually, to Berkshire Hathaway, a company making billions of dollars each year, might reflect the conduct of their respective stockholder meetings. There is something to be said about the respect for stockholders and employees when it is coupled with leadership and common sense, as it appears to be a very profitable combination. When the Annual GM Stockholder Meetings resume, I suggest the Chairman and CEO conduct the meetings in a more professional manner to all the attending stockholders, as they do deserve to be treated with utmost respect. It's about time GM act like a company that cares and is pleased to listen to comments and answer to the stockholders' questions. After the 2007 stockholders meeting in Wilmington, my wife sent a letter to Wagoner and suggested they move the meeting back to Detroit for the convenience of stockholders.

In the 1980s, General Motors held their annual stockholders meetings in the Detroit Fisher Building. When GM started losing billions every year, the meetings were moved to a difficult-to-get-to location, the DuPont Hotel in Wilmington, Delaware. It was one surefire way to keep GM employee attendance down. At the time of the location change, most of GM's Employee Stockholders lived in the Midwest (GM towns).

Interestingly, Ford also holds its annual stockholders meeting in Wilmington, Delaware.

SAME OLD ... SAME OLD

I do care about what happens to the American auto industry, but the recent changes at the top only mean some of the flies have changed, but the manure is still the same. Both Ford and General Motors are living in a short-term, bottom-line culture of the past. It may take a going-out-of-business situation to change the spiritual/cultural environment—bankruptcy for General Motors sure didn't do it.

THINGS ARE LOOKING UP

The June 7, 2011, GM Stockholder Meeting was a stark contrast to the hostile exchange between past GM Chairman and GM shareholders. The new GM Chairman, Daniel Ackerson, had a much calmer demeanor that made communications with shareholders better.

About 80 GM stockholders showed up. I usually sit up front next to Ms. Evelyn Davis. She was scheduled, but she did not show at the last minute. Reverend Jesse Jackson came down and sat in the front row with us retirees, waiting to make a presentation to the GM Chairman.

I presented the following to Dan Ackerson and the GM Board of Directors:

- Creativity and Yankee Ingenuity chapter
- The Lease/Recycle Program chapter

After the 1 hour meeting concluded, Dan Ackerson walked off the stage and came directly to me and thanked me for my input. I asked if he would like a copy of my report. He said yes, and handed me his card. Anne Larin, Corporate Secretary for General Motors also gave me her card. The GM Chairman mingled and talked with a number of stockholders; he did not use the side exit to escape like all chairman have done in the past.

I mailed Dan Ackerson's requested information the next day.

Never in all of my years of attending the GM Stockholder Meeting have I ever seen the GM Chairman come down to talk to stockholders on a one-on-one basis. To me, it appears that Dan Ackerson is just the people-person to bring the spiritual leadership solution to General Motors. Lee Iacocca was able to provide the spiritual leadership that Chrysler needed in 1980.

All in all it was a pleasant day. It was the most sensible GM Stockholder Meeting I have ever attended and everything ended on a positive note. My wife Jan and myself would have planned to attend the June 15, 2011, Ford Annual Stockholders meeting, but it is to be inconveniently held in the Hotel Du Pont in Wilmington, Delaware.

SPIRITUAL LEADERSHIP FOR THE AUTO INDUSTRY

The automotive business is a technology business, run totally by people who know nothing about technology, that is the problem. —Retired Automotive Engineer

It's ironic is that a crisis like the Detroit Three recently weathered is probably the only way they could've gotten back some of their groove. Former Chrysler CEO Lee Iacocca and the late UAW President Doug Fraser both concluded as much when they worked together during the company's government bailout in 1979-80. Yes, worked together. But then they were exceptional leaders who saw Chrysler heading down the tubes unless both sides made major concessions. Ever since then, there has been a dearth of outstanding leaders in the Detroit Three management and in the UAW, with the possible exception of Mulally, former GM Vice Chairman, and product guru Bob Lutz.

Now heady with their newfound rosy outlook —"Pendulum Swings Back Toward Detroit" proclaimed a recent *Wall Street Journal* headline—the U.S. automakers are armed with a $2,000–$3,000 cost advantage over their Japanese rivals according to David E. Cole, Chairman-emeritus and founder of the Center for Automotive Research (CAR). However, there remain endemic management shortcomings that must be addressed if the Detroit Three are to withstand the extreme economic upheaval I predict is coming in 2012.

THE "FROZEN MIDDLE"

> When everyone thinks alike, then no one thinks at all.
>
> —Del C. Schroeder

The "frozen middle" was a term coined by Roger B. Smith, GM's CEO in the 1980s, to refer to GM's solidly entrenched middle management. What he observed were middle management executives so preoccupied by going to meetings they had very little time for thinking, much less thinking creatively. Midlevel executives always wore their suits to work because it was their emblem of rank and achievement. Dark navy suits with a white shirt and a red tie were known as a power-suit, according to John T. Molloy, the author of *Dress for Success*. Whenever I had a meeting with anyone in financial, I always wore a gray pinstripe suit, vest, and wingtip shoes. I guess I was just messing with them because I had already worked six years in financial at the Cadillac Motor Division; I spoke the language and knew the dress code. In the 1980 to 1990 timeframe executives were called "suits." Actually, the executive dress code in the auto industry was not much different than a U.S. military uniform.

Viewing management from my position as an executive in what was called the "frozen middle" was actually a reality. To me, the position became one of posturing and maintaining status quo. Once the executive position was achieved, some people just plodded along, adapting to their new office setting and trappings. Lunch in the Executive Dining Room; a company car washed and kept filled with gas every day, and parked in your assigned spot in the Executive Garage.

> One of my offices had a desk speaker-phone with a little red button on the back. When I questioned the telephone repairman what the red button was, he told me it connects\ed directly to plant security, and once pressed it would have a security team in my office in less than three minutes. The office was previously occupied by an executive who dealt with the UAW. I had the button disconnected.

Executives were provided a 18- by 18-foot office, with a bulky desk backed by a wall-to-wall credenza and a meeting table with six chairs. A large plant was the standard of the day.

Each executive had a personal secretary who handled all telephone calls, took dictation, and handled office correspondence and filing. When I ordered coffee I always brought one for the secretary, so she would feel part of the team. Over the years, as I changed positions, I have worked with many fine secretaries who seemed to have clairvoyant capabilities like Radar on the TV program "MASH."

With all of those perks, executives felt that maintaining business as usual was all that was required. One engineer described a true "yes man" as someone who'd agree with your next statement before you said it. Many who got promoted were "yes men," not team players, and were seen by the people who promoted them to be in their spitting image.

There have been some successes. Former General Motors CO Jack Smith presciently pushed GM into China in the 1990s, and it's now that nation's largest automotive manufacturer. GM also can reclaim some technical brag points with its plug-in Volt electric hybrid and re-designed Buick, Chevrolet, and Cadillac models. Under CEO Alan Mulally, Ford recently has rolled out a phalanx of eye-catching, high-mileage cars and trucks and escaped bankruptcy by wisely borrowing cash before the 2008 meltdown. Chrysler, which has had more lives than the proverbial cat, has begun a turnaround under Fiat/Chrysler CEO Sergio Marchionne. They made a profit in the first quarter of 2011 and planned to pay off their U.S. government bailout loan in mid-2011. Fiat is injecting technology into Chrysler's products while re-establishing the Italian automaker's brands in the U.S. market. All of these developments were spurred by the crisis that enveloped the industry, commencing with Wall Street's financial meltdown in 2007. Perhaps the biggest loser is the UAW, whose membership is now one-fourth what it was at its highest. The union's givebacks have gone a long way toward matching the labor costs of foreign transplants operating in the U.S. and it's paying off as the resurging Detroit Three hire new and laid-off workers.

The frozen middle was created by bosses who kept promoting people just like themselves who would adheres to the corporate line, handle their executive job assignments exactly like their predecessors, and not make waves. It always amazed me how little innovation and visionary leadership came from the higher ranks.

One GM division had a reputation for lacking any semblance of being innovative. Engineers joked that anyone working there claiming to have "thirty years of experience actually only had one year's experience—thirty times."

Some executives liked to think they should serve as a "Devil's Advocate" to solve problems. To me a devil's advocate is nothing more than a dream-stealer and a demoralizer, and should have never been promoted into a leadership position in the first place. Executives should be selected based on their visionary leadership skills, not on just their judgmental skills. Other executives were promoted not based on ability, but because they were old college buddies: an unusually high number of executives came from the same company-supported schools.

LEADERSHIP WITH VISION

It is the lack of leadership, a spiritual leadership of vision and trust, that is the main factor holding the American auto industry back—and dragging it down for some time now. Employees and customers are looking for vision, trust, pride, passion, purpose, persistence, honesty, integrity, and respect with principle in their leadership. And that is what it's going to take to revive and rejuvenate the workforce. Outstanding and courageous leadership to provide and keep to Strategic Plan goals will straighten this mess out.

I see a hired CEO from the outside more like a gunslinger, hired by the town fathers to come in and straighten out the town. A gunslinger is hired to do his job; after doing that job he collects his money and leaves town.

What we need is an all-American, Jack Armstrong-type leader with Boy Scout values. In this day and age, they just don't make them like they used to. Anyone looking at a top job in the auto industry today will want stock options in the $50 million range. That's well over 600 times the average UAW worker's annual income! How does a CEO with that kind of compensation even relate to the hourly workers?

There have to be leaders willing to work for a reasonable compensation package. I know the amount of money in the package is how executives keep score, but it needs to be done within reason. That special person is out there, one that puts the value of the company and the country above personal values.

Conveying the Spiritual Message

Ford and General Motors' leaders must insure that Vision, Trust, Honesty ,and Integrity are practiced and flow easily throughout the entire corporate culture. When there is no Vision, Trust, Honesty, or Integrity, then everything else becomes meaningless.

TRUST is the main part of the spiritual problem within both organizations. Leaders can tap the intellectual capital (brain power) of the workers by offering them respect, dignity, and honest practices through TRUST. When TRUST is instilled, leaders can inspire the inner power of others to contribute and propel the last two, true American automotive companies into a competitive future.

With effort from the right leadership, Ford and General Motors can be fixed, but it is going to take a lot of work before they're on the road to a successful future. If the people who work in the auto industry do not trust their bosses, then by deductive reasoning, neither do the customers. Trust, beginning in leadership, is the most important element to restoring the greatness of the American auto industry.

PERSONAL VALUES

Lee Iacocca originally came into the Chrysler organization as a hired gun to turn the company around. But once Lee put Chrysler on stable footing, he stayed to the mandatory retirement age of 65 after being with the company 14 years.

A retired Chrysler executive of Body Engineering was impressed by Lee Iacocca's leadership during the Chrysler bankruptcy. Lee was honest, he said, and when each executive made a list of employees to be laid off, he promised, "We will put them all back on the payroll as soon as we can." Lee was true to his word, and all laid-off employees were rehired within a year. Further Lee would meet with all Chrysler executives once a week to give a company status update so they could relate the information to their employees. This retired executive gave me the impression that he felt Lee Iacocca was a true leader with integrity.

TRUST = STABILITY

In the early 1990s, space shuttle engineer Roger Boisjoly was brought into GM as part of our Creativity Series to speak to over 500 engineers about ethics. Boisjoly believes TRUST is the most important ingredient responsible for the ultimate success or failure of every corporate business endeavor.

Boisjoly's experience in ethics stems from testimony he gave before a Congressional hearing on why the Challenger fuel tank seals failed. Boisjoly tried to stop Challenger from lifting off on January 28, 1986. But NASA officials pressured Morton Thiokol's management to approve the launch. Boisjoly refused to give in and he was over-ridden by management. The launch was approved. If Morton Thiokol's management had trusted Roger's evaluation, seven lives could have been saved and a disaster and scientific setback to the United States space program could have been averted. (The National Geographic Film Documentary on the 30th anniversary of the Challenger disaster pivots entirely around Roger Boisjoly and his testimony.)

Trust

by Roger Boisjoly, retired rocket scientist

Everyone must realize they have two crucial and critical responsibilities every minute of every day.

1. Always encourage, to the point of demanding, to have subordinates always tell you what you have a need to know, and this means and especially includes bad news, concerning the corporation's vehicles.

2. Always tell your bosses what they need to know, so they can use their power to take ownership of the problem. It is mandatory for everyone to maintain a two-way trustworthy communication, no exceptions.

TRUST IS NOT ROCKET SCIENCE! My charge to every future American automotive employee is to practice proper organization behavior. Employee treatment is, in reality, all about trust and common sense. When TRUST is restored, everyone in the corporation will be pleasantly surprised to see that it works and it will provide long-term stability.

Trust is universally based on truth, honesty, integrity and respect demonstrated by reliable people.

PART FIVE

SUMMARY

The United States has been drifting into a nation where the moral and social values have continued to deteriorate because we try to be almost everything for everybody. We are about to become both morally and physically bankrupt through poorly thought-out fiscal policies and illegal immigration issues. At our current rate of borrowing, and with $1.4 trillion in additional debt each year, the United States will soon be in a position where it can't even help itself.

It is time we pull ourselves up by the bootstraps...It's time we help ourselves before it's too late.

A STRATEGIC PLAN FOR SAVING THE LAST, TWO GREAT AMERICAN AUTOMOTIVE COMPANIES

Key Steps to the Plan

- **Combine both Ford and GM's technical departments of Design, Engineering, Manufacturing, and Research and Development resources to enhance their chance for survival.** The newly consolidated technical group will now be able to compete head-to-head with its rivals from overseas. The new group will share technology across the board for the betterment of both companies just the way technology was shared in WW II.

- **Focus on fixing the Spiritual Problem.** The American auto industry is in a life and death struggle and there is no room for political correctness! Find qualified men or women who understand automotive technology and who can really do the job. Get the MBAs out of operational management positions because they don't know "Jack" about technology.

- **Ford and General Motors must be led by creative, visionary leaders.** Find individuals with a technical backgrounds who have spent most of their time in operational and product release positions and understands automotive technology. The following virtues establish the character of the corporation. Leaders must insure that Vision, Trust, Honesty, and Integrity are practiced and flow easily throughout the entire corporate culture. Respect for the truth is the formation of the morality for the corporation.

- **Establish QUALITY as the main issue that provides value and excitement for the customer.** Build vehicles using 24 Sigma Quality Control Methods. Quality must be engineered and factored in at the inception of part design.

- **Ford and GM must project a message that all of their vehicles are becoming cleaner and more fuel-efficient every day** because visionary engineers are again running the companies. Every day these issues become more important as oil supplies are costlier and their use is polluting the planet with greenhouse gases.

- Develop vehicles that have an excellent appearance, remain in style and still have value before the vehicle wears out.

- **The U.S. Government needs to establish the Department of Industry and Technology (DoIT).** As a nation, we need to stop the de-industrialization America!

- **Ask every American with a driver's license to submit ideas to the (Ford and GM) Yankee Ingenuity Program.**

- **Develop a Marketing, Sales, and Service Plan to support a Lease/Recycle Program.** Establish a 100% Lease/Recycle Program goal by 2016.

- **If there is a future stimulus, I encourage every American citizen to support the U.S. government to include stock in true American Automotive Companies.** This way every tax-paying American citizen would become a stockholder of both Ford and General Motors.

- **Make certain that every Ford and GM investment is an "investment for the future".**

Establishing this strategic plan will allow for the survival of the last, two American automobile companies as one, otherwise they are LIVING ON BORROWED TIME.

PONTIFICATION

PREPARE FOR THE NEW WORLD ORDER

When both India and China emerge onto the world stage, everyone in their path will be flattened by their industrial power. In 2006, China graduated 60 engineers to every 7 in the United States. Think what the ratio of engineering graduates is today. The United States will not have the ability to compete in the next ten years if it doesn't do something now.

Advancements in technology in India and China will create a total un-certainty for workers in Europe and the United States within the next five years to a decade. Up to this point, the development of India and China has provided a great economic benefit to American businesses. U.S. companies have moved manufacturing operations overseas for tax purposes and for the maximization of profits for their stockholders (and personal compensation), but at the expense of the United States government, the American worker, and the ultimate consumer of their products. It's about time the United States government, Ford, and General Motors—the last, two American automobile companies—and American industry in general change things before it's too late. Unemployed workers purchase nothing!

When is the U.S. government going to wake-up and realize the only way our children and future citizens can compete with the newworld order is through education? This message should be supported by both Ford and General Motors because they are always looking for educated employees.

This "Importance of Education" message should also be pushed on Facebook, because any child with access to a computer is on it. In plain English, as a nation we have to get the importance of education in their faces. To me, soft messages in Facebook would be the ideal method to get the "Importance of Education" message to our children. Include video games for children that focus on education. (Example: Engineer vs. Janitor and their life-styles as a puzzle game.) All children love to play video games and they learn from them. Develop a series of educational puzzle games that show the value of getting a better education. It is also important as parents and grandparents to encourage our children and grandchildren to become educated, creative, and productive Americans. To put it into a better perspective, "Life is hard; it's harder if you're stupid." —John Wayne.

THE UNITED STATES GOVERNMENT DOES NOT HAVE A CLUE

When I say the United States government doesn't have a clue, I'm not saying the people who run our government are not smart or even brilliant. Many of them are what I would call "educated fools." According to the urban dictionary, an educated fool is a person filled with book knowledge but lacking in common sense. Being educated and having common sense leadership skills do not go hand in hand, and the U.S. government has provided living proof of total incompetence for the past 50 years.

It is about time some one question why the U.S. Military's primary job is to keep peace in the Middle East and the oil flowing, when we are not the major benefactor. It is hard to believe that no one in Congress noticed the billions of dollars spent by U.S. taxpayers to OPEC when we use U.S. solders lives and U.S. money to protect the OPEC oil routes. Yet the U.S. citizen pays top price for oil and pays for protection too. Sounds STUPID to me.

Why not impose a higher CAFE and force Americans to drive more efficient vehicles? Does Congress placate the U.S. citizen as a spoiled buffoon who always gets his way just to get elected?

Most people in government seem to lack integrity, wisdom, vision, and the common sense leadership skills needed to run this once great nation of ours. I make that statement based on the actual proof of how the American citizens were scammed when the government put their Social Security funds into the nation's General Fund (because the government was spending more money than they were collecting in taxes) way back

> It is a thousand times better to have common sense without education than to have education without common sense. —Robert Green Ingersoll

in 1963. And nothing has changed in the last 48 years. That is why the U.S. government is trillions of dollars in debt today. It's all due to a lack of integrity, wisdom, and visionary leadership.

Today the U.S. government is claiming that there are not enough funds for Social Security because of an aging population. If the funds had been held in reserve, generating income for the last 48 years, the Social Security Fund would not be bankrupt today.

In 2011, Congress has not only frozen Social Security payments in inflationary times, but is now considering cutting Social Security benefits as a way to help balance the national debt. Congress has the gall to blame Social Security recipients for living too long as the reason for payment problems. No one in Congress will admit that the U.S. Congress over the years borrowed 1.7 TRILLION DOLLARS from the Social Security Fund without any intention of repayment. If the congressional retirement plan was Social Security just like everyone else, I'm sure Congress would be much more prudent in how they spend Social Security funds.

The American auto industry was being run by similar people—it is infested by MBAs, people with a Master's degree in Business Administration. MBAs are trained to focus on short-term results, not quality, which has been the downfall of the American auto industry.

GM filed for bancruptcy in 2009 because they ran out of Divisions to sell. To me, it looked like GM was running a Ponzi scheme for the last 21 years just to stay afloat.

Back in the 1990s, a GM executive was so frustrated with top management, he stated, "Those guys who are in charge of General Motors aren't capable of grabbing their ass with both hands." To put his mind at ease, I gave him my personal 8" x 10" print in the GM colors of blue (Truth) on a white (Purity) background. It came from Mark Twain, "Is this place being run by Geniuses who are putting us on, or by Imbeciles who really mean it." I kept the print in my top, center desk drawer and have used it many times to put my mind at ease when questionable decisions were made.

I think those same remarks also apply to the federal government. Even at the beginning of 2011, U.S. government officials without integrity said there was no inflation because food and fuel costs are not figured into the inflationary index. DUH! Isn't the cost of food and fuel at least 50% of the American household budget today?

The Labor Department created a special index called the "Chained Consumer Price Index" (CCPI). The CCPI was created to measure the actual cost of living for the American family. In February 2011, the CCPI reached an all time high, surpassing the high of 2008.[1]

The Cost of Living Adjustment (COLA) is currently frozen by Congress. Yet Medicare insurance premiums have increased in 2009, 2010, 2011, and yearly increases are scheduled through 2014. All Social Security recipients are dealing with a frozen COLA for 2011, and the cost of living is going up. Congress is either composed of educated fools or government officials without integrity? Take your choice.

The need for oil and the de-industrialization of America has redistributed our country's wealth to the Middle East and Asia. This redistribution of American wealth is what is leading up to the financial collapse of America. The reality of life is that the United States cannot borrow forever, and the time to pay the piper is coming. In the end it will be the American Public's gluttonous appetite for oil and the automobile that is bringing this once great nation of ours down to its knees.

---

1 *Fast Money;* 3/17/11.

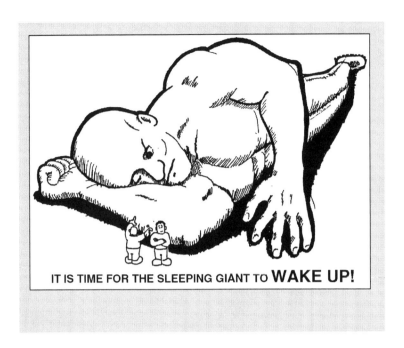

IT IS TIME FOR THE SLEEPING GIANT TO **WAKE UP!**

Like it or not, as a Nation the United States is morally and financially bankrupt! A matter of fact, even Dallas Federal Reserve Bank President Richard Fisher stated in a speech at the University of Frankfort, "The United States is approaching insolvency—the only question is when."[2]

Based on the past performance by Washington politicians who refuse to vote in established term limits, it is time to throw the whole bunch out. We need leaders with integrity (who care more about the nation than personal power), wisdom, vision, and common sense to lead this nation out of the rat hole we find ourselves in today. It can be done, but it won't be easy.

When I look at the Middle East situation, I find it most puzzling when I wonder about the real reasons why the U.S. went into Iraq and Afghanistan, wars that each cost the United States billions and billions of dollars each day. In 2000, 2001, and 2002, Saddam Hussein was selling Iraqi oil to some European block countries directly for euros without using

2 Reuthers; 3/22/2011.

the World Reserve Currency (the U.S. Dollar). When talking about the

World Reserve Currency, there are over a trillion U.S. dollars in circulation around the world as paper and in electronic trading. If those dollars ever come home to roost, the United States as a nation would be broke. If the U.S. Dollar had been dethroned as the World Reserve Currency before the 2004 presidential elections, I do not think George W. Bush would of ever been re-elected. Someday, the world will find out if the euro was the real weapon of mass destruction that could of destroyed the U.S. economy back in 2004.[3]

President Barack Obama in his Presidential Address of 22 June, 2011, stated that over 4,500 U.S. Military personnel had lost their lives in Iraq, plus the tens of thousands of U.S Military personal injured or maimed, and I question, for what? I find it a total hypocrisy, to waste U.S. Military lives and destroy families, spend billions of dollars each day just to protect the dollar and power in Washington. Think of the U.S. solders killed or maimed in Afghanistan just to secure the land for a oil pipeline in the future. Billions of U.S. dollars spent each day just to gain access to oil reserves for Big Oil. What's wrong with this picture?

Jan found this article on the Afghanistan Pipeline: Google; *Is an Oil Pipeline Behind the War in Afghanistan?;* Oct 15, 2001. It pertains to a proposed oil pipeline through Central Asia that is applicable to the current war in Afghanistan. So, in 1998, Osama bin Laden was identified as the villain behind the Taliban; Afghanistani women the victims of an oppressive Taliban regime; and the stage was set for a future stabilization effort (i.e. a war). Was all this a cover story for a future oil pipeline? In a ten-year timeframe the CIA and the military could not find Osama bin Laden. But maybe once a decision was made not to build an oil pipeline in such a hostile land was established, it was the correct time to take out bin Lauden and withdraw from Afghanistan.

---

3 *Time*; 11/13/2000.

Everything relates to political expedience.

I consider myself a very lucky person to have lived in the United States in the 1960s. When I worked at General Motors, it was at its pinnacle of success, and the U.S. government was a superpower and lender of money to all the world. Those were the best of times. Now, 50 years later, everything is upside-down. In 2009, two of the former Detroit Big Three auto firms declared bancruptcy and the United States has become a debtor nation. The U.S. is borrowing over a trillion dollars each year just to keep up the "superpower" status, without any plan for repayment. The United States will soon be facing default, just like Greece.

I predict the first depression of the 21st century will be America's Golgotha. I feel sorry for those U.S. citizens just entering their careers under such financial uncertainty.

Many people reading this book will think that I'm very opinionated. Yes, maybe I am, but in reality, I'm also expressing the thoughts and opinions of many of my friends and colleagues who represent the silent majority. I'm speaking out for all of those Americans who are afraid that the United States is in the process of sliding into a financial abyss.

For a reality check, ask your personal friends how they feel about the situation the United States is in today? Also, sound out friends on how they feel about illegal immigration, the survivability of industry, and the American auto industry—see if they even care?

We are at the point where the silent majority is fed-up with the politically correct do-gooders who are spending American tax dollars to provide welfare from Social Security funds to dishonest citizens and illegal immigrants.

To me, this nation is at the decision point... Does the United States live or die as an industrial nation? The decision is up to our elected officials in

Congress who represent the American Public. If we as the voting public do not contact our senators and representatives to force the issue, then the failure to succeed as a nation will be entirely ours and we will have no one else to blame.

The United States of America is only 235 years old and still a work in progress, so it's time for all of us to get off our collective backsides and get to work.

God Bless the United States of America.

Del C. Schroeder

ACKNOWLEDGMENTS

To Jan, my loving wife and sole mate for being so patient, and I want to thank her for her loyal support in helping me finish writing this book. I am forever in love with her.

I want to give special thanks to Heather Shaw. Heather's advise was most helpful on sections that needed to be re-written for clarity. Heather is a genius! Website: www.heatherleeshaw.blogspot.com

In my many conservations with James K. Paisley over the years have stimulated me to write this book. I thank Jim for his honesty and thought provoking strategic planning input.

I would like to thank Roger Boisjoly for his essay on trust and integrity in the work place.

I want to thank Jim Dollinger for the marketing chapter. Jim Dollinger is the founder of GeneralWatch.com.

An appropriate thanks to all the people who gave input to me personally and on the website: lookoutamerica.org.

A special thanks goes to all the readers of this book for understanding that I was only able to capture a few ideas that can change the American auto industry. Hopefully these ideas will stimulate many more, and create a ground swell of ideas for the people in charge. We need to stabilize and grow industry and also the American auto industry which creates real income paying jobs that are the foundation of the American economy.

BIOGRAPHY

Del C. Schroeder grew up in Algonac, a small Michigan town located on the St. Clair River. He had a normal childhood with a sister and loving parents who encouraged him to participate in anything creative. Because his parents noticed that he had a lot of creative energy, they guided him to build things.

At the age of 12, Del built his first plywood kit boat that he raced in the Algonac Racing Association, and supported his boat's racing expenses by being a *Detroit News* carrier. Del became an Eagle Scout at the age of 14. In High School he played football, track and hockey. Algonac, was the birth place of both Garwood and Chris Craft Boat Companies.

Even though his parents were college graduates, his mother was a stay-at-home mother and he grew up in a lower middle class to middle class income environment. He learned how to save and made sure all bills were paid on time.

Because his mother was born in Belgium and came to America when she was 2, that makes Del a first generation American. It is the first generation Americans who have worked hard to prove they are worthy citizens—legal immigrant parents instill that work ethic.

As a youth, Del worked on a farm that grew fruit and vegetables, and later worked in an upscale restaurant in the 1950s to save money for college. Del had to pay his way through college the same way his father did; they both worked and bussed dishes for their meals. Del's dad went to the University of Michigan, and so did his son. Del went to Michigan State University majoring in mechanical engineering and transportation design. Del is also a proud member of Triangle Fraternity, a social and professional fraternity of engineers, architects and scientist.

When Del built his personal sports car the AURORA, he pushed himself to have the body completed in just three months, working 15 hours every day.

Del has always been fascinated with the Renaissance period, the men of that day were engineers, sculptors, painters and creators of mechanical war machines. They were men for all seasons. After engineering, Del's art career became secondary in an effort to balance his goal of obtaining a Renaissance background. He also did graduate work in Nuclear Engineering. Del always felt that nuclear power would become an automobile power source by the year 2000. Boy was he wrong, because light weight radiation shielding has not been invented yet.

During his career, Del had the opportunity to work in a variety of job assignments. Each job assignment was chosen to provide a broad range of experience to become a better engineer someday. Del was an executive for 15 years of his 32 year career at GM in a variety of engineering and manufacturing assignments.

Over the years, Del coached Little League Baseball and youth hockey. In the 1990s, Del was Co-Head coach for the Birmingham, Michigan "AA" High School Hockey Team. When Del retired, they began to give the "Coach Schroeder Award" to the hockey player with the most tenacity. Del did not coach for pay—to him it was a civic duty and a way of giving back to the community all of the benefits he received while growing up.

Del's automotive career started at GM Styling, then Cadillac Financial, Ford Research and Scientific Labs., GM Advanced Manufacturing, GM Truck and Coach Body Engineering, GM Truck and Bus Manufacturing Engineering, Executive in Charge of a GM/DuPont Joint Venture, GM CPC Division - Advanced Vehicle Engineering - Chief Engineer Pontiac Stinger, GM CPC Division Manufacturing Engineering and a contract engineer for Chrysler Research and Advanced Engineering.

His 51-year working career encompassed a variety of experiences. Del has always operated on the principal that "IMPOSSIBLE, WAS AN OPIN-ION—NOT A FACT."

In the course of his travels over the years, Del has been granted a total of 27 U.S. automotive patents through the GM and Chrysler patent system and they are the property of the respective corporations. Del also shares a patent with his wife Jan on a marble boardgame. Today, Del is an engineering consultant using good, old "Yankee Ingenuity." Del has derived a lot of enjoyment in working with people doing creative projects.

Del's sense of accomplishment has been in helping others accomplish their goals. So many people have helped Del as he progressed through life, his debt and gratitude has been in helping others achieve their goals.

Proof

Made in the USA
Charleston, SC
30 June 2011